"Wendy Ida's *"UNBREAK ME: Pus* *Resilience & Reclaim Your Strength"* is c .... and most prescriptive books I've read on the prickly subjects of lost love, aging, and emotional and physical wellbeing. Using powerful stats, stories, and insightful wisdom, Wendy wrote this from her heart, mind, body, and spirit . . . plus years of research and thought as a long time physical and mental activist. *UNBREAK ME* is revealing, warm-hearted, instructive, and sobering. If you are at all curious about jump-starting your life again this is a rich source of insights and solutions. And yes, it's a great year-round read, but start now, there is no time to waste, we have a lot of catching up to do. Thank you, Wendy, for this masterwork."

Dr. George C. Fraser
Chairman and CEO of FraserNet, Inc.,
Author: Success Runs In Our Race and Click

"They say you hear the right words at the right time. *Unbreak Me* has arrived! Wendy Ida delivers the words that build confidence, give hope and truly inspire! Prepare to transform your life!"

Cindy Popp
Producer/Director
The Bold and The Beautiful

"If you are feeling lost in life, you've got to read this book! With Wendy Ida as your guide, you will gain the confidence, the hope, and the mindset you need to go from broken to unbreakable!"

Rickey Ivie, Esq. | Director
IVIE McNEILL WYATT PURCELL & DIGGS

"We all have undesired life experiences that erode our thrill of living or bless us with deep healing and transformation. We all are barraged by life-defeating messages about aging that we allow to diminish our resilience, vitality, and passion, or that we defy to become wiser and more energized. I personally experience Wendy Ida as a living example of the vast amount of resilience, vitality and passion that we can retain as we age. Her book, *Unbreak Me*, doesn't waste your time with useless platitudes about what to do -- it combines "love talks" and micro moves" into powerful prescriptions for how to do it. If you value building your thrill of living as you age, infuse yourself with Wendy's magic starting today."

Dr. David Gruder, PhD, DCEP
The 12-award-winning bestselling Human Potential Strategist,
Business Lifecycle Psychologist, and Societal Wellbeing Catalyst,
who was named America's Integrity Expert

"If you are going through a challenging time in your life, Wendy's own triumphant story combined with her specific tools, processes and strategies will equip, strengthen and give you the resilience to begin your own journey of authenticity and change. You will be empowered to develop a winning mindset, achieve your goals and manifest your wildest dreams."

Constance L. Arnold, Host
Think, Believe & Manifest Talk Show
Law of Attraction Radio Network

PRAISE

"If you're at the place in your life where you feel stuck – stuck health wise, stuck weight wise, and therefore, stuck in your life – Wendy's journey is one you need to hear! No matter your age, and especially if you're not 25, or even 35, Wendy has the secret that will get you out of your rut, and into a new life and a new you!"

Felischa Marye
Producer/Showrunner/Director
HI FELISCHA! PRODUCTION

"This is a wonderful book to read over and over again. Wendy is an inspiration to us all. Her drive, determination and positive attitude is contagious."

Susan Haber
President Haber Entertainment

"When you think you've been broken beyond repair; that all that's left is to throw in the towel; that there's no way back—you're wrong. Wendy was there and made it out, as many others have. In this book and her other media, Wendy now helps others fight to win against whatever life throws at them."

Bill Duke

7 TIPS TO LOOKING FIT FIERCE, AND FABULOUS

Includes: 7 Minute Circuit Workout

GIVE ME 20 MINUTES
AND I'LL GIVE YOU THE TOOLS NEEDED TO TAKE YOUR BODY AND LIFE TO THE NEXT LEVEL.

I created this e-book and video because I want to help others improve their lives, live their dreams and serve the world through their passion. To make the kind of impact I'm talking about and to serve a greater good, it's important that you be **FIT, FIERCE, AND FABULOUS!**

This FREE e-book and video could be a blessing in disguise! You can't afford not to know this. You have to take action to make things happen!

https://bit.ly/FitFierceFabulous

Unbreak Me

Push Beyond Fear, Gain Resilience, & Reclaim Your Strength

Wendy Ida

Dedication

*To all my family—thank you for your support and
for putting up with me when I get extra hyper.*

*I can't help it, lol. It's all because you
make me happy, and I love you!*

*To my children Sky and Tre'—I'm so proud of you and
the people you've become. I did a good job considering
the challenges. Keep going strong and remember . . .
your potential is always bigger than your problems.*

*And last to my dad, Harold "Pop Pop" Rollins. As a
musician, you were never home, and I missed you dearly.
You missed so many of our daddy daughter dates.*

*But I am thankful today that you've made up for it. You've kept
your promises, made apologies, and said I love you. Three
simple words I was longing to hear from you all my life.*

This daddy's girl loves you back!

Contents

CONTENTS

Foreword

We owe it to ourselves and to the world to heal and grow into the best version of who we are meant to be.

I've spent decades helping people create their best selves through nutrition and healthy living. Nothing is more gratifying than to see someone leave the pain of their past behind and step into a future bright with promise.

To make that happen, a journey of mind, body, and spirit is required. Navigating that process requires courage and brings clarity and wisdom. It's not an easy transition, and we are forever changed by it.

While we make that interior odyssey in the solitude of heart and mind, we don't have to go alone. A map and a wise guide can make all the difference, encouraging us during the most difficult moments, making sure we don't lose sight of the goal, helping us to believe in the process and in ourselves.

In this book, my friend Wendy Ida has created both a map and a guiding voice to lead you through a process of transformation. With vivid imagery and clear insights, she provides a step-by-step process for making the healing journey of a lifetime. She shares frank insights from her own experience, demonstrating a deep level of understanding that is only gained by having traveled the same path.

You're about to embark on an adventure of mind and heart that will change and challenge you. You'll dig deep to discover the power of resilience, gratitude, forgiveness, and courage. As you face fears and release old secrets, you will discover a fresh, amazing future waiting for you—and Wendy will be your guide every step of the way.

It's time to become who you were meant to be, and become your true self.

—Dr. Tony O'Donnell, PhD

Introduction

You don't know me. I mean the real me. And sometimes I feel so alone. Felt that since I was a teen. It's funny how you can be in a room full of a crowd of people and yet feel a sense of loneliness. Sometimes it feels like I'm on another planet or living in another universe. It's a feeling of raw nothingness swirling around in the pit of my stomach. There's no doubt you come into this world alone and you'll go out alone. But to live it alone is another animal.

I mean alone in your head—feeling misunderstood. It's like the ghosts of your past have their way with you and spit you out, and those experiences linger on and on and become a part of you. It becomes a part of the decisions you make, the dreams you dream, and the feelings you feel about yourself. It becomes a potpourri of cloudy thoughts that makes it difficult to differentiate the good from the bad. Sometimes you give in, cower down, and do nothing. You live in fear. And it becomes the norm because you're trying to protect yourself, but it prevents you from really living and feeling and being your true self.

Broken is the feeling I felt—broken and alone.

Have you ever felt that way? If you can relate, you know how serious and destructive it can be to live that way. That is one of the reasons I was inspired to write this book. At different points in my life, I have felt all of those things, and I've spoken to many others, including my clients, who have felt the same way. Maybe I can help you understand that there is a better way to cope and surpass that feeling of brokenness—one I've used for myself that has been very successful for me.

The world wants to tell us that we're too old, too lazy, or not good enough to be worthy of everything that life has to offer. That's not true! Don't believe the hype! No matter where you are in life, how old you are, or how far you need to go, you can take your life to the next level and make all your dreams a reality. You don't have to be afraid, and you never have to go back to feeling broken again—like I was. You are worthy, you are beautiful, and you are more powerful than you know. I intend to show you how to use that power.

People look at me and ask, "How did you break world records, become a lifestyle coach and fitness expert, and speak all over the world? What did you do to look so good and feel so great at your age?" I tell them it was a process, and I'm revealing that process to you in this book.

The truth is, I didn't always want to be a bodybuilder. I was broken for many years, eating fast food and holding onto negativity that was bringing me down. That moment, when I escaped my old life and started my new one, was the beginning of a long, long journey to where I am right now.

At some point, I remember thinking that I had pulled it all together. Have you ever felt like you're on top of the world, life is good until suddenly, it isn't? Something surprises the hell out of you and knocks you sideways so you can't see. I mean, it breaks you all the way down, breaks your spirit, breaches your confidence, and stagnates your motivation to live. And you don't know how to handle it. That was me too. We all have to go through many changes in life that test us—more than once, twice, or three times. I've lost count. Regardless of how many times life changes and bad things happen, here's what I know. Sometimes you win, and sometimes you learn. I've learned that the trials and tribulations we experience are purely a test of your character. It's meant to strengthen you and provide wisdom.

From the time we are born, we are preparing ourselves to live life in a manner that can help you live in grandeur—to be happy and thrive! But how do we get out of our own way to deal with the monster that has grown within us? How do you own your mistakes, bad judgments, and wrong choices? How do you forgive and take control of the things that got out of control? How do you deal with the regrets that still cause you great pain and live respectably on this planet?

Maybe you're at a roadblock right now. Maybe you're looking at this big problem in front of you, wondering how the heck you can get around it and keep moving forward with your life. You might feel overwhelmed, afraid, or even nervous, but as long as you don't give up, you will get to the other side. Resilience is about not giving up. Throughout this book, I'm going to give you my formula for building resilience.

Never Give Up!

We are going to take a long journey together. I will challenge you, motivate you, and drop some truth bombs. In the end, it will help you push through your fears, build strength, feel confident, and you will find your power as a result.

Keep in mind that transforming yourself isn't about grand gestures or big steps. The tiniest step forward can make a difference. Review the lessons often to build strength and let go of the negativity that's been weighing you down. It's not going to happen overnight. But it will happen if you don't give up. Just be consistent and follow my roadmap.

It's the same as weight loss or anything else. Rome wasn't built in a day, and I didn't lose eighty pounds, win awards, break records, and write books overnight either. I had to use the power within me to get rid of negative energy and generational curses I had been dragging around with me for my whole life. I'll show you how to do the same thing, so you never have to feel broken again. Even when my entire world was crumbling down around me. I didn't give up, and you don't have to either.

I learned how to unbreak myself, and I'm going to share those skills with you so you can do it too.

After you uncover your strengths and empower yourself with the skills I am going to share with you, the possibilities in your life will be endless. I'm not saying it will be easy, and I'm not saying life won't get tough because it always does. What I am saying is that you will be able to push through the tough stuff. You will become stronger than you once were. And you will be equipped with the ammunition you need to get through anything that comes your way. Those tools will give you the resilience you need for the rest of your life and that only will bring you much joy!

We can do this together. So, let's go!

PART ONE

Resilience

WENDY'S WISDOM:

*It's often the deepest pain that empowers
you to grow into your highest self.*

CHAPTER 1

Life Will Bring You to Your Knees

"Whatever brings you to your knees in weakness carries the greatest potential for your personal success and spiritual victory."

—Charles Stanley

For forty-two years, I was dead.

True, my eyes were open. My arms moved; my legs moved. My chest seemed to rise and fall like other women all over the world. My mind contained an entire ocean of thoughts.

But I was not really alive; my light had been extinguished a very long time ago. In fact, I felt like I was dead, and no one knew. Silently, inwardly, I grieved for the girl I had once been and the fantasies of my life I thought I would never realize. My resilience, if you can call it that, was simply getting out of bed every day. At the time, that was all I could manage. That, and the love for my children. That was my whole world.

As a woman and as a mother, I can say with confidence that the worst feeling in the world is to look at your children and know you cannot protect them. To know with equal certainty that they are in danger and there is nothing you can do. It is the kind of help-lessness that comes when all of your power has been taken away from you. When you have been so beaten down, so accustomed to the abuse that you no longer even flinch at the blows. It is an awful feeling, and it was my reality for the thirteen years of my first marriage.

One question that is always leveled at the victims of domestic violence is, "Why didn't you just leave? Why didn't you get out the first time it happened?" To someone who has not experienced that situation firsthand, it's natural to perceive the situation as black and white, utterly clear and defined. However, the reality is anything but. Abuse, more often than not, does not start with a dramatic display of violence. It's like the proverbial frog placed inside the pot; at first the water is only lukewarm, but by degrees that temperature starts to rise until it becomes scalding, intolerable, even deadly.

My first marriage was a campaign of psychological and physical warfare, abuse, and manipulation. And it might never have changed had it not been for a vision I had. I'll never forget. It was 11:00 a.m. on a Sunday morning, and we were driving to church as we always did—my husband, our two kids, and me. I was sitting in the passenger seat, as I always did. I felt like a zombie, as if I was comatose and watching someone else's life through a hazy fog. My husband was drinking beer and smoking dope as he drove us to church—the same as he always did. My babies were in the backseat crying like they always did.

"Mommy, Daddy! I don't like the smell! I can't breathe!"

I couldn't say anything; I couldn't do anything. If I tried to stop him, I would be punished severely. So, I listened to my children in pain and buried the hatchet in my soul, cursing myself for my inability to act. For my weakness. For my fear. It was the regular

4

list of hateful thoughts. And then all at once it hit me, like a building dropped on my head—this *had* to change.

I dropped to my knees in that car, and I cried out to him, "Please, please stop, for the sake of the children."

My husband looked at me with murderous intent before shouting in my face. *"I will do whatever the hell I please, and you can't do a damn thing about it!"* And he was right. I could do nothing about it at the time. Then he gave my five-year-old son a swig of his beer, and that's when it happened. I snapped! My mind left me for a moment, and I saw a horrible vision of my children's future— one I knew I couldn't live with.

It was as if I had woken up from a bad dream, only to realize that I was living in a nightmare. I can only describe it as one of those out-of-body experiences, the kind where the entire universe seems to hit you with intense clarity.

That was my breaking point!

I had to get away. That's where my resilience first started to sneak in. Of course, I didn't call it that at the time; I just realized I had to take action for the sake of my babies. They were my motivation. They were my lifeline.

I had tried to escape before, but it didn't work. Before, I didn't have a plan. I didn't know what I was doing, and I didn't go far enough. The last time, my then husband had caught me in the act and forcefully dragged me out of the car. From that point on, I was on twenty-four-hour watch by him and his family. I was a flight risk, as if I was a deranged criminal. So, even as the weight of this profound realization hit me, I knew that getting away from this man would take every ounce of my perseverance, willpower, and determination.

I knew the time would finally come to make my escape when Sunday rolled around again because I knew he was going to church.

He was like the devil himself, dressed in his Sunday best. Whatever else the man was, he knew exactly what my buttons were and which ones to press to keep me from leaving. He would often take one of the kids with him, knowing full well I wouldn't go anywhere without both of them. And on that day, he tried to do the same, telling me that my son was going with him to the service. It almost failed; my plan was almost defeated before it ever began. He was stepping out for ten minutes and before he left, he said that the kids and I had better be ready to go.

I was scared to death. My heart was pounding hard, my hands were shaking, and I was crying. I knew this was my last chance— it was my last chance to get away for good—so I had to make a break for it.

My window of opportunity was ten minutes. That's all I had to grab a few survival things, shuttle my children into the car, and literally run toward a new life. Ten minutes—no more, no less. The moment he stepped over the threshold of the door, I held my breath and waited silently for three minutes in case he forgot something and had to return. Then I whirled around the house like a manic tornado, throwing items indiscriminately into a bag for me and my children to camp out in for a couple of days before our flight was due to take off.

My children were wailing, sobbing, and screaming in fear the whole time. Just looking at my crying eyes and wild emotions made them more fearful. I knew this was going to be terribly traumatic for them, and even through the fear and adrenaline, I wanted to find some way to console them. My children needed comfort, something to keep them feeling safe. For my daughter, it was her doll. That was her safe place, her refuge. I hurriedly grabbed it and gave it to her. Then later stuffed it into her pack, letting her know that it would be there for her when she needed it. Because for now, we just had to get to that car. My son, however, wanted his dog. I knew that wasn't possible; there was just no way we could bring him along.

I grabbed my children in one hand and an arm full of things in the other and jumped in the car. As we sped away, they were both crying hysterically in the backseat.

"Mommy, mommy, I want my dolly." And my son was yelling that he needed his dog; he couldn't leave without his dog. It was heartbreaking, and I just kept repeating, "We can't bring him with us; we just can't!"

I could see their frightened little faces in the rearview mirror, and their cries tugged at my very soul. I thought surely they deserved to have some little piece of comfort and security through all of this.

I got to the stoplight, and I thought I can keep going straight or turn around. Keep going straight or turn around. The light turned green . . . and I turned around. I drove back to the house. The dog was just out of the question, but my son does love his drum set.

I'm driving back toward that nightmare of a home just to run in there and get a drum set—not even the whole thing, just a piece of it. I know that my son needs something from home, something to feel safe. But before I even got out of the car, I saw my husband was coming for me! I saw him and another car pulling up— my husband's family's car—looking for us. I almost died at that moment. I didn't hesitate; I hit the gas. The tires screeched loudly.

I took off like a bat out of hell. I was screaming, sweating, praying, and shouting, "This is my last chance." My heart was pounding out of my chest, and my children were out of control. It was like a scene from a movie.

This time, when I looked in the rearview mirror, I saw him. I saw his car; I saw his face. I could not let him catch me this time. I zigged and I zagged, I ran red lights . . . and I don't know how, but I got away. I never got that drum set or my son's dog. But I *did* get my son, and I *did* get my daughter.

Have you ever felt like you have been brought to your knees? I know you have. Everyone has a breaking point.

Everyone has a point when life brings you to your knees where turning back is not possible. Think of an airplane without enough fuel to turn back. That was me. I was out of fuel to return to my abusive husband. I also knew I was out of chances; if I stayed, I would die.

I'm talking about those low, low points in our life. Those moments when we feel like we can't go on. Those moments when we feel like our lives are out of control, and we're not worthy of moving forward. We might be brought to our knees by individual trauma, collective trauma, or years of being dragged down by the pressures put upon us.

People describe this as their "rock bottom" or their point of no return. It's often the deepest pain that empowers you to grow into your highest self.

There are many reasons this happens.

We feel the pressure of balancing our careers with motherhood or being a good partner and provider.

We find ourselves isolated and alone in a global pandemic.

We find ourselves at a certain age, being told that we can't do various things or be the person we have always wanted to be.

I say "we" because I've been there too! I know the challenges that come with the transitions of age. I know the challenges of being a mother, sister, daughter, and wife.

Women—especially women who are mothers or care for their families—are the backbone of the world. And we are a spine that is often tested—bent, broken, knocked down, and pushed aside. I've been there. I've been broken every which way and expected to get back up and be the best mother and father, career woman, and everything else. Today, I'm living my best life, but not because anything was handed to me on a silver platter; it's because I've pushed through the tough times and didn't give up on myself.

Looking back, I can't tell you how many times I wanted to quit and throw in the towel. So many times, I felt trapped, hopeless, and out of gas. I can't count the number of times I dragged my feet, barely able to put one foot in front of the other. The fights, the threats, knocking my lights out, choking the hell out of me until I had no breath, the drugging me against my will—all of that. I have to shake my head and pinch myself because sometimes I can't believe I'm still standing on planet earth. Every time I talk or write about it, I remember another piece of my life that I had conveniently and intentionally shut out to not feel the hurt and embarrassment. I am *so* glad I didn't give up. My children's lives would have been so different because I wouldn't be here to save them. My gut and intuition say so. And I trust my gut.

Life will bring you to your knees at some point in your life. Maybe you feel like you are there right now. If you feel like this, read on.

If you want the tools to give you a stronger backbone while you tackle your greatest fears and emotional traumas as you lift up your partners and your family, all while feeling secure and more confident in yourself, read on.

If you are one of those people who doesn't finish what they start or gets thrown off track easily and you are looking to get unstuck, read on.

People also ask how I made it through the worst times of my life and how I'm able to smile today, win competitions, write best-selling books, earn Guinness World Records, and more.

"Whatever brings you to your knees in weakness carries the greatest potential for your personal success and spiritual victory." Charles Stanley said it best, and that is how it's happened for me. I'll never forget my past, but I vow to never suffer like that again.

I remember the fear when I had ten minutes to escape my former husband. It gripped me to the core. It gives me the shivers as I think about it now. Fear, lack of confidence, and not feeling worthy held me down and stopped me from breaking free for way too long. I was afraid I wouldn't live much longer with him, but I also feared that I couldn't make it on my own. That's what fear is—a double-edged sword. Fear will push you onto your knees and then tell you that you'll hit yourself on the head when you get up.

Fear nearly suffocated me and took my life on several occasions. With all the domestic violence stories I've heard, I am fortunate to be among those who made it out alive.

How did I push through that fear? My children were the catalyst that sparked a flame in me at the time, then I got support from family, friends, and therapy. It was a process, and things didn't change overnight; there was a lot of trial and error. But I didn't take "no" for an answer. I kept trying different ways to make life better for my family and me. With each move, I gained a little success and more confidence and courage; I began to understand my power and worth. I'm still a work in progress, but light-years better than I once was. I started understanding that I have another chance at success, dreams, love, and joy, as long as I don't give up. Each time I pushed through something difficult, I got better at it, and I became less afraid to try it again. Yes, I fell on my face and got bumps and bruises along the way, but I kept going. I didn't know it at the time, but I was exhibiting signs of a really good foundation for what it means to be resilient.

My intention is to share with you the strategies I've learned to help you understand your worth, help lift you up where you belong, and give you the same formula I give to my clients, so you don't have to work so hard at finding all the answers. These tools have helped me push through my fears and emotional traumas and taught me to be proud of who I am and never give up.

So, these days, just call me the Energizer Bunny because I'll keep going and going and going. I owe it all to the fact that I made one small move at a time that changed my life forever.

That's what I want for you!

CHAPTER 2

The Real Superpower

"Resilience is very different than being numb. Resilience means you experience, you feel, you fail, you hurt. You fall. But, you keep going."

—Yasmin Mogahed

Holy crap! I made it! We made it! My children and I made it up high in the sky to safety. Lord knows, that's when I finally exhaled. It was the first time I had felt safe in fifteen years.

As I've said, there were so many times where I wanted to give up and give in, and boy, I'm so glad I didn't. My life today is too good to have potentially missed so much! We were blessed with the opportunity to live again.

That was my third escape. The first two times had failed. But I kept trying, and each time I learned something new and used it to help me the next time. The fact that I kept trying and didn't give up were positive signs of resilience. I was resilient for my children. I escaped for the love of them. They helped me get up, day in and day out, no matter what abuse I had suffered.

The What and Why of Resilience

Resilience is the secret to navigating life's many challenges. It's a necessary trait that can and must be learned and applied to survive difficult experiences in life. It will not only help you cope with the tough stuff, but it will also help you recover from life's hard realities.

Resilience is the ability to push through any obstacle no matter what. It's a test of character and strength. Resilience is a necessary ingredient to live a happy, healthy, and fulfilled life at any age.

Ultimately, it means developing an attitude and mental framework focused on a core belief. "Whatever I do, I will NEVER GIVE UP. I will see it through to the end."

Happy, healthy, and fulfilling lives don't always look the same year after year. Our bodies change, our situations change, and we have to change with the world around us. Resilience gives you the ability to love and accept your self-image as it changes.

I'm talking about all types of changes, good and bad. I'm talking about failures, obstacles, and being knocked down to the ground. Many people fall short, get thrown off-track, or stop entirely because of the hurdles, hoops, and obstacles they have to climb over just to survive. The only way we can cross the finish line is by tapping into our resilience. It's the ability to get up and move forward repeatedly after falling or failing in life. The remarkable thing is that resilience brings with it an opportunity to learn and grow.

There are three key pillars of resilience:

◆ Resilience is mental because it's the ability of an individual to adapt to mental health adversities.

- ◆ Resilience is emotional because it's the ability to adapt to stressful situations or crises without lasting difficulties.

- ◆ Resilience is physical because it's the ability to keep moving, one tiny step at a time, even when you don't feel like it or are in excruciating pain.

Part of having resilience is truly looking at yourself. I mean, going *deep*. So many of us define ourselves by roles, standards, or expectations. We can't see past our gender or our salary or where we grew up. You have to look past the labels and rules that people have put upon you.

Resilience is important because it enables us to develop mechanisms for protection against experiences that could be overwhelming. It helps us maintain balance in our lives during difficult or stressful periods and can also help us deal with or avoid mental health issues.

When we cope with stress in a positive way, we gain many health benefits, such as lower rates of depression and greater satisfaction with life. As you develop into a resilient being, you gain positive traits like emotional well-being, inner drive, future focus, and physical health. With each positive step you take toward becoming more resilient, your confidence grows and therefore, you take more risks. Your energy increases and you want to do more, be more, and take care of yourself better. As a result, this keeps you motivated, hopeful, and excited about your future.

Where Does Resilience Come From?

How do you start telling yourself that you are resilient—that you are important and special because of who you are? You have to cut out all the noise and the chatter and listen. Listen to your gut.

Listen to your intuition. This is the first step in recognizing the resilience you have within you.

Just like you, I was born with that gut feeling that pointed me in the right direction. I didn't know that I was tapping into a part of me that represented embryos of resilience. I just thought it was my mother's voice swirling around in my head.

When I look back, I can see that my resilience has always helped me make good decisions. At age nineteen, I decided to go to New York on my own. I had gone through modeling school, put a portfolio together, and was ready to make it big. I got off the bus with the guidance of my mom and auntie in my ear and thank God I did.

If you've ever stood in front of an agent or casting director, you know how important it is to listen to your gut. Many of the men I spoke with during that trip just wanted to take advantage of me and other young women trying to build their careers.

Before I went to New York, my mom warned me about this. Her voice was echoing through my head when a man approached me on the street. He knew every modeling agency on my list; he seemed to know everything about the industry. This man convinced me to sit down and have a drink with him. I was promised everything under the sun—he would introduce me to his business partner; I was going to get all of these fancy clothes, blah, blah, blah.

I asked him if we could make an appointment—the other agencies and directors had made appointments with me—but he said no. He told me his partner was in the hotel across the street, and they would sign me right there.

Bells were ringing in my head! Alarm bells! Mommy's bells!

I walked away from this man because my mother's voice got louder in my head and told me not to go. And when I made that decision, this man threw all types of cuss words at me. He was screaming at me from across the street at the top of his lungs! Thank God my mom's voice screamed when it did. If I hadn't heard my mom and my gut telling me to walk away from this man, I might not be alive to tell you the story today. Had I not paid attention to that deep gut feeling, I might have taken this man up on his offer. My intuition tells me that he was involved in human trafficking, or worse. He was a monster ready to lure in any smiling young woman who didn't know any better. I did know better, and because I listened to what I knew, I'm alive and well today.

Even though I got lost along the way and my self-worth was torn apart, I was eventually able to build back up to where I am. The most precious gift through my journey is that I found me, and I found the courage to live the life I deserve and go after what I want. I've learned to trust my instincts. With that, you can do anything and go anywhere!

My resilience was nurtured by people like my mom and my aunt who showed me how valuable and important I am. It's nice to have role models, but you don't necessarily need role models to build up your resilience. If you didn't receive guidance in your upbringing, it's not too late. As long as you're breathing, you can learn skills to help you develop that resilience.

What Stops You from Being Resilient?

One of the primary things that throws people off track and stops them from being resilient is trauma—but not just major body trauma like losing an arm or a leg. Trauma is more far-reaching than that. Trauma can be mental, physical, emotional, and financial. It accumulates over time if not healed, and its effects can last an eternity.

Physical trauma can be large or small; broken bones, deep cuts, or even health conditions like cancer can be an enormous blow to your resilience.

Mental and emotional trauma come from events that shake your confidence: body image issues, loss, bullying, discrimination, or abuse. These events shake your world until you don't know which end is up. You lose your sense of who you are.

Experiencing trauma of any kind has a physiological effect and can leave an imprint on your body as well as your mind. The reactions you develop to cope with trauma—healthy or not—are passed on to people in your family who witness how you react and experience the brunt of unhealthy or toxic coping mechanisms.

Psychology is just now beginning to understand that traumatic experiences can actually change our brains and our cells and those changes can be passed down from generation to generation.

So, if something terrible happened to your grandparent and they never dealt with it effectively, their behavior and the physiological changes in response to trauma left a mark on your parents. If they didn't deal with that traumatic baggage and continued to model unhealthy or toxic coping mechanisms, their response and the cumulative brain and body changes also left a mark on you.

Breaking that cycle of a particular trauma affecting your body is essential to stop intergenerational "curses."

Shared Trauma

We have all experienced shared trauma during the COVID crisis. We can pretend the effects are gone and try to go back to the old normal, but we still lived through the pandemic. So many people have lost family members. I lost a cousin to suicide—COVID pushed him over the edge. Following that, his brother died of a heart attack. Other family and friends died or were affected in different ways because of COVID. We all know people who were affected.

But even those of us who have survived the pandemic suffer massive uncertainty. Political and social unrest will continue if the underlying cause has not been addressed and solutions put in place. When nothing changes—nothing changes. When the world feels like a never-ending dumpster fire, we suffer emotionally, mentally, spiritually, and physically even though we have minimal control over the big issues. That stress and collective trauma doesn't go away just because we can finally go down to the local bar again to get a drink. Trauma leaves an imprint on your body and mind.

For two years leading up to the pandemic, I had a lot of personal drama and life changes going on. When the pandemic hit, along with the political unrest in the US, followed by Russia's attack on Ukraine and everything else going on in the world, I felt like I took on not only my personal traumas and issues but also everybody else's. That's a perfect storm for a mental health crisis.

I witnessed the George Floyd murder on social media live in real time. As I watched, I cried out several times for the perpetrator to let him go. And I found myself gesturing, trying to make the officer take his knee off Mr. Floyd's neck. My heart pounded, and I held my breath. I could sense this was going to be really bad. It felt like a family member's life was being sucked from the earth before my eyes. I felt so helpless. Now I can't unsee the image in my head—EVER! I can't unsee the brutality or his death. It was so traumatizing. I had nightmares that night.

Witnessing that incident increased the drama I already had going on and deepened my feeling of being in crisis. Everything was coming at me all at once, and it felt like it was going to take me out.

Doubled Down Trauma

As they say in Vegas, I doubled down—or life doubled down on me. And it caused anxiety to the point where I checked into the emergency room on two occasions.

My heart wouldn't stop racing. I had headaches, body aches, and panic spells. At times, my spirit took a dive. That part was really scary. Other personal and family issues were also happening in my life which I'll tell you about later. So it felt like I was being pummeled emotionally.

I had some of the best medical people working on me, and both times, my tests came back negative for any serious conditions. The doctor was perplexed because he couldn't find anything wrong, and I remember saying, "Look, I'm not crazy. I know what I felt, and you have to believe me." I couldn't believe all this could happen to me, but it did!

We don't get to go back to the same world that existed before the trauma occurred. We are changed, the way we see the world changes, and neither can be undone. That's a *big* deal because these traumas have a very real effect on body, mind, and spirit.

That's why recovering strength and confidence after trauma is not just about physical workouts. You have to address all of you. And while it's essential to stabilize the mental and emotional parts of you, to have any longevity and resilience, you have to go beyond that to pour yourself into a *thrive* mentality. If the mind and emotional self aren't right, you will cut your life short. And the opposite is true—when your mind and emotions are healthy, you extend the health of your body in so many ways.

A healthy body is not all about how you look on the outside; it starts from within. And resilience begins with how you think.

I did a lot of work on these issues during the pandemic, both for myself and for my clients. I also had a therapist help nurse me back to health mentally and emotionally because I had so many stressors hit me all at once. Living through a pandemic is not a normal time for anyone. We have all endured hit after hit from the upsetting events we've seen in the news, whether or not they personally affect us.

Uncertainty

One of the hardest things to cope with is uncertainty, and we've had constant uncertainty during the pandemic on political and social issues. When something actually happens, you can brace yourself to deal with it. But when multiple very scary possibilities remain likely but don't ever resolve, you end up staying in a constant state of high alert that takes an enormous toll on your body, mind, and spirit.

For the same reason, you shouldn't feel ashamed if you lost or gained weight or if you are out of shape because the truth is that you experienced a trauma you had no control over. You couldn't dodge it, you have limited personal control, and all the stress and changes to daily life affect your body and psyche.

The good news is you're still here, and you can adjust for it.

Like many people, I gained weight (about twelve pounds) during the pandemic. Although I shed it five months later, nothing has rocked my world like that in the thirty years since I lost eighty pounds and learned to love working out—the start of my fitness and life-change journey. So, I'm the same as you. We all fall short when facing overwhelming, unending stress we can't directly control. It doesn't matter what your level of education is or what kind of job you have. No one is immune.

The key is—don't let it stop you. Grow and apply what you've learned to keep building your story toward the conclusion you want to see. That's what I've done every time the world knocks me for a loop, and as long as I never give up, I eventually get where I want to go.

Working through trauma is hard, but you can do it. If you try to unpack everything that has happened to you or affected you all at once—or even *think* about unpacking it—you might feel overwhelmed. And feeling overwhelmed can make it tempting to walk away entirely and never face what has caused the problem!

Digging up Roots

When I talk about "unpacking" the trauma, I mean dealing with the root cause head-on, not just trying to make the symptoms disappear. Think about having a suitcase filled with all the things that have hurt you in the past, the things you're most afraid of, and how you might have been disappointed or betrayed.

You drag that suitcase with you everywhere you go, and it smells terrible. Just touching it makes you feel sick. But you can't let go of the suitcase until you open it and clean out what's inside. Some things in the suitcase happened to you directly. Some were passed on to you because they happened to parents or grandparents who never unpacked their own suitcases and left the mess for you to clean up.

Unpacking the suitcase is scary. It means looking at each rotten, moldy item inside one by one and facing how they affected you and made you feel. It can involve learning difficult truths about yourself and the adults who raised you. But once the suitcase is empty, you don't have to be afraid of the contents anymore. They no longer have power over you. You are finally free.

Dwelling on whatever's worrying you instead of taking action to deal with it and move on leads to looking for ways to numb the pain and anxiety. Those can be unhealthy behaviors like drinking, drugs, and eating junk food. But it can also be overdoing good things, like compulsively exercising or obsessively tracking everything you eat. These coping mechanisms give you a feeling of control that may feel good in the moment, but they won't help you get up and moving day after day. They distract you from taking the steps necessary to make real change and push through trauma.

Second-Class Trauma

The pandemic, political unrest, economic difficulties, and social unrest don't exist in a vacuum. They've made us much more aware of how our systems were strained and broken even before the events of the pandemic years.

Experiencing micro aggressions, rudeness, and inconsideration in small moments can also disrupt your ability to be resilient. Years of facing racism, ageism, misogyny, homophobia, and other forms of discrimination create cumulative damage, like water dripping on rock and eroding a hole. Mental and emotional anguish and second-class treatment can traumatize you, just like significant, single events.

Resilience is a mindset that develops over time, which helps you adapt to difficult situations and react in healthy and useful ways to trauma, adversity, and tragedy. Resilience in the face of unremitting discrimination feeds the will to get back up and keep going. As resilience develops within you, it also builds confidence and reduces stress.

Natural Life Changes

Resilience isn't only a response to trauma; it can also be valuable with any major life change, including aging. Aging can mess with your mind and stop even healthy people in their tracks! The reality of reaching your forties, fifties, sixties, and above can test your resilience. People find that the changes that come with aging, both in their physical body and in the world around them, can shake them up! Aging gracefully is actually a form of resilience. But that's not an easy perspective to learn, especially when we live in a culture that emphasizes youth and doesn't value maturity.

Many of us are dealing with this *simultaneously*. We're aging, changing, watching our babies leave the nest, going through a divorce, caring for our elderly parents, having to find a new job—that's a lot to deal with! You need a strong sense of resilience to get up every day and fight for yourself. That's difficult under normal circumstances, and nothing about the COVID years has been normal.

A big first step toward gaining resilience lies in taking action. You might not be able to fix a national or global problem, but you can speak up at a meeting, sign a petition, have a conversation—these actions all help you do something with the trauma you felt instead of sitting and feeling helpless.

A Core Problem: Lack of Resilience

One way to build or increase resilience is to look at who you think you are and how much you're defining yourself by the roles you play in life. Who are you, aside from your roles and titles? What do you think makes you unique?

If you don't know who you are outside of your money, status, looks, gender, family connections, and relationships, you are letting those external pieces define you. More importantly, since you don't control those pieces or rely on someone else to provide them, they can be taken away.

Knowing who you are outside of those elements creates grit—a deep-down stubborn knowledge of self that refuses to be silenced and can't be stolen. You are important and special because of who you are, not because of those external factors.

Do you ever wonder why some people stop short of their dreams, while others keep going and achieve everything they've ever dreamed of—including some of the things you've mentally kicked around as being goals for yourself? You guessed it—resilience. People who have developed resilience can clear any hurdle, hoop, and obstacle in front of them. They will run, jump, swim, and climb to reach their dreams. They just keep going until they cross the finish line.

But not everyone can do that. In fact, a lack of resilience is at the core of some of our biggest societal problems. These problems don't always look like a resilience issue, but when you dig a little deeper, you see the connection.

Some people are hung up on their value because of a particular title at work, job position, or a big office. But when the job goes away, they feel like a deer in headlights and wonder, "Who am I now?"

That was me when my children had all left home for college. As an empty nester, I had no clue who I was outside of being a mother. I've heard the same story from my clients. Some people who retire don't know who they are or why they're important because they aren't the job or the title anymore, and they don't have a special parking place, corner office, or the other status perks.

When you can say to yourself, "I am worthy and exceptional just the way I am." you are onto something bigger, better, greater, longer-lasting, and more resilient than ever!

Resilience is huge! It has the potential to change the world and improve our society. Later in my life, I started to recognize that my gut feelings and motivation are part of my resilience. I saw that as long as I kept trying—even when I failed—there was hope of accomplishing my desires.

Hope is the beginning of faith, and faith takes you a long way. It keeps you steadfast and strong when everything is going wrong or life feels unbearable. I have faith that you, too, can strengthen your resilience, despite everything life throws at you, and I believe you can overcome any problems that you have yet to face.

How Do You Gain Resilience?

I didn't recognize what resilience was when I was escaping my abusive husband in New Jersey. As I have looked back on my life and the many times that I tapped into my resilience, I can see there is a formula to building resilience that you can start using today.

Each of us has the power within to push through life's roadblocks and become what we desire because the truth is we were all *born* resilient. As newborns, we lay on our backs until we feel strong enough to roll over and crawl. Toddlers fall down a lot when learning to walk but get back up again and again. They want to walk more than they are held back by fear of failing—or falling.

But depending on your life experiences, the skills that reinforce resilience can be stripped away and torn down or they can be nurtured to build you up and increase your resilience.

You've got to take risks to see what is possible to create, or you will regret what could have been. You have only two choices—take the risk or lose the chance.

"The biggest risk is not taking any risk . . ."
—Mark Zuckerberg

Remember—you instinctively know how to master what you want to do in life. You've got resilience in you because you were born with it.

The reason we stop being so resilient is fear. It's a natural desire to protect ourselves and the fact that some people in our lives may actively undermine our resilience and beat it out of us to control us is sad. They teach us to fear, punish our failures, tell us we can't do something, belittle our abilities and successes. Regaining resilience means unlearning those toxic lessons.

Fear of the trials and tribulations in life cut us so deeply that we lose faith in ourselves. We doubt we can push through and go the distance or do what we desire. We fall down and think we can't get back up.

We get lost and feel stressed because we can't seem to find our way when really, it's a matter of relearning the natural resilience you had as a child. It's not easy retraining yourself when life gets in the way and you've been scared, but it's definitely doable. It takes practice and repetition to get better at it. But it's worth it to make life meaningful and find joy while reaching all your goals and dreams. You just have to develop the habits and skills to let your natural resistance shine through.

Throughout my life, my resilience skills were nurtured in small ways—and sometimes in very unhappy ways that I've since corrected or adjusted after therapeutic advice.

For example, one of my coping mechanisms was to numb myself and act like whatever terrible thing happened didn't happen. I'd do this when my father would disappoint me by not showing up on our daddy-daughter dates. I'd be left in the window like a puppy looking for him for hours, tearing up, feeling empty, and very sad. To get over it, I would wipe the event from memory and tell myself not to depend on anyone. Sheer rebellion enabled me to build myself up and feel better from the sadness and emptiness. I felt strong by saying, "I'm going to show him that I can do better." But later, I mistakenly put faith in my abusive husband.

Over the course of my life, I got lost several times, but each time, I came back to the thought that I didn't want to disappoint myself. I would lock away the memories that made me feel sad or disempowered or afraid. While that got me through in the short term, I am still uncovering some of those buried thoughts and feelings, which is therapeutic for me. You see how messy life can get? I've had highs and lows and I have gone back and forth trying to find my way to make life better. But there's no shame in my game and there shouldn't be in yours either. That's life.

What you do every day counts toward your big life goals, and how you do it along the way affects your journey. The skills you use along that journey determine your measure of resilience. It starts with one step, one life, and one person at a time.

The thing that really counts is hanging in there to have any chance at winning the fight. Whether we are talking about fitness, finances, food, family, health, love relationships, or business, most people want something great and long-lasting. They want *resilience.*

To be resilient, you have to have courage. Courage means being afraid but doing it anyway. Courage is wanting to change your life so badly that fear doesn't stop you.

When was the last time you showed courage in your life? You may not have fled an abusive relationship, but I know you've had moments where you have been courageous, which means the courage is within you. *You* have the courage, and *you* must pull that courage out from deep inside you to make the changes you need to make now!

To be resilient, you have to trust your own creativity. When we get exposed to new things, our creative wheels want to turn. If you can trust what those wheels are creating, you'll be surprised by the solutions you come up with.

Creativity will keep you motivated, challenged, and young at heart. When you feel stuck in a rut, creativity will help you get out.

To be resilient, you have to find an outlet. Have a trusted place where you can talk through the changes you are going through and the roadblocks you are facing. I'm not talking about hosting a pity party! I'm not talking about venting about how tired you are! I'm talking about speaking to a trusted mentor or confidant who will guide, encourage, and troubleshoot with you. Find someone resilient in their own life who believes in you, with the confidence that you can strengthen the resilience in your life.

To be resilient, you have to nourish and hydrate yourself. Our immune systems suffer when under stress and enduring physical, mental, and emotional trauma. We have to supply our bodies with good nutrition to persevere. Most importantly, we have to stay active. Cardio and strength training will prompt your body to release endorphins—and endorphins are the leading fighter of stress!

When you put these together, you will feel a renewed sense of well-being just like a superhero. Your strengthened resilience will make every part of you come alive again, from your head to your toes! That's how it happened for me. I felt dead for forty-two years, but once I tapped into my resilience, I came alive again.

I have given my kids, clients, and myself a second chance. Now it's your turn—give yourself a second chance and a new beginning!

I know making changes is not easy, but nothing in life is easy. You have to trust what your intuition is telling you right now. That's the beginning of mastering the art of resiliency.

Micro Moves to Gain Resilience

Our culture feeds on this whole idea of "go big or go home," but guess what? You don't have to. "Go big or go home" is a lie. Don't let these lies hold you back from taking smaller steps because those smaller steps do add up.

Our culture likes to tell you that famous people are an overnight success; actually, they have often been working their butts off for twenty years and got a lucky break. The media sells their story as if one day they walked out of their house and became a celebrity. And we buy that story because we don't like to think about all of the long nights, rejections, and setbacks they encountered before they found success. Rip that story up! Throw it in the trash! To change your life, start with small steps.

And it's okay if you don't think you're strong enough to be resilient day in and day out. You don't have to be! Sometimes, small steps are all you can do. But you know what? Those small steps will get you through the next hour. They will get you through the next day. Again, all I had was ten minutes to escape my first husband—but I got through those ten minutes. If you can get through the next hour, you can get through the next day, the next week, the next anything!

That's how I've lived my life and got to where I am today. It didn't happen overnight as some people seem to think. In fact, take anyone on the planet who has any measure of success. If you look at where they started, most of them achieved their goal through small steps and gradual increases.

I call these small steps micro moves, and I will be referring to them in every chapter because it's really important to gaining resilience. Micro moves create micro progress and, over time, can have a compounding effect that ultimately adds up to achieving big results. Micro moves reduce stress and fatigue and help create valuable lifelong habits.

Micro Resilience

When you experience failure or trauma that makes you feel anxious, fearful, or hopeless, or days when you feel you can't go on, the secret is to take small, strategic steps toward a resolution that will empower you. I call it micro resilience. That is how you will see the change in your life!

For example, micro resilience is when you tell yourself that you really want that piece of cake, but you decide to wait an hour before eating that. If you still want it in an hour, you can have it.

Sometimes you will totally forget about the cake, or it doesn't sound good anymore. In other cases, you really did want it—not just eating to reduce stress or for something to do. But you made yourself stop and consider. Often, you'll end up not eating the cake, which is great for your fitness goals!

So, if you don't think you're strong enough to be resilient, just take today hour by hour or minute by minute to build strength. Sometimes that's all you've got. Tell yourself, "I will get through the next hour."

When we fall short and things happen, we often get deflated, and our problems seem so prominent in our minds that we become overwhelmed. This can be resolved by taking small strategic steps.

The first course of action is to remember why you started your journey in the first place. Post a note in your bathroom mirror or in a conspicuous place so you can't miss it. That will remind you to keep going and help you discover and build on the resilience you were born with.

Name Your Trauma

After a bad experience, we really want to tuck it away and forget it ever happened. The problem is that you can't fix what you don't acknowledge. When we don't recognize our trauma, we risk repeating the same behaviors that don't serve us.

To move forward, you have to be aware of what your trauma actually is. Give it a name so you can work with it, realize it, and fix it. In order to move out of a place where you feel stuck, it's essential to face yourself in the mirror and leave all the excuses and rationalizations behind to figure out the truth about what is really going on. Gather the courage to discover what you're feeling, and that first move of naming your trauma will guide you toward where you are meant to go next!

Change the Story You've Been Telling Yourself

Change up the bad stories about yourself that you repeat in your head. Here's the old story: You may have gotten upset in the past when things went wrong. Bad decisions and hurt feelings snowball downhill until you are constantly beating up on yourself, and it makes you feel like a failure! Self-deprecation, sabotage, fear, depression—they have all been a part of your story for a long time.

Here's your new story. When you mess up, fall down, or miss the target, repeat to yourself, "I am not a failure. I am brilliant, powerful, and worthy." Remind yourself that these opportunities are another chance to get things right, do better, and become more creative.

Every time you catch yourself repeating the old story in your head, follow it with a positive phrase. "I am strong. I am lovable. I deserve the best. I am capable of creating enormous success in my life." Rehearse this story daily until it becomes automatic and a part of who you are. I promise—it will!

Surround Yourself with Strong, Positive People

The reality that surrounds you is the one you create. Do you want to be surrounded by people who want to bring you down or people who lift you up? Arm yourself with people who will hold you up when you need to be strong. This is about creating the resilience you want to see in your life. When you're surrounded by positive and strong people who believe in you, you will eventually come to believe it too.

Today could be the beginning of your new journey. If you've felt dead inside for longer than you can remember, it's not too late to wake up and start living right now. Start with my micro resilience moves, and I assure you when you look back in a month, a year, or ten years from now, you'll be glad that you made the decision to do so.

CHAPTER 3

Gratitude Is the Attitude

"Be thankful for what you have; you'll end up having more. If you concentrate on what you don't have, you will never, ever have enough."

—Oprah Winfrey

When the plane landed in California, my sister was there waiting for me with open arms and tears in her eyes. She was so happy to see me and know I was finally safe. Although my heart had been pounding during the flight because of the uncertainty of my future, when I saw my sister and her kids, I felt the love and that pounding started to slow down. I had to slow down. To pick myself back up, I had to step back, check out the environment I was in, and see where I fit in!

This took place in small moments. I remember so many nights, I would step outside and just look at the stars. Man, that sky was so blue! Where I came from, the sky was always grey and dreary. Or maybe that's just how I saw it. Here, I had hope. I had a chance to come alive again! I was going to spend every day underneath a big, beautiful blue sky.

I took stock of everything that had changed around me. I was in a new place. The homes were different. Even the air seemed different. The people, the way of life, everything was so different. And you know what? I was so grateful. Grateful that I had made it to California. Grateful that I had made it out alive with my children and grateful that I had another chance at making a better life. I walked around at night asking myself, "How did I get so lucky?" In hindsight, I know it was grace.

And then I would just breathe.

I would take a big breath in and let a big sigh out. In and out, in and out. I would look up at the sky and thank the stars, the moon, and the light that I was in California with my sister. In that space, at that moment, I knew I was exactly where I was supposed to be!

It felt like my eyes were being opened for the very first time, and I could see the natural goodness and stillness of life that I had never seen before. I remember clearly that it was the start of showing sincere gratitude and seeing how it worked within my life.

I still do this today. I walk outside, look around, and just take a deep breath. I take in that blue sky above me, and I feel the glory of being grateful for where I am and how far I've come. It was eerily close to what my mother would always say. "Take time to smell the flowers." This small practice I developed was healing. *Gratitude is so healing.*

Defining Gratitude

People often trivialize the idea of gratitude, but gratitude is not a simple, Pollyanna goody-goody thing. Gratitude is a big part of building mental strength.

When we express gratitude and receive the same, our brain releases dopamine and serotonin, the two crucial neurotransmitters responsible for our emotions, which make us feel good. They enhance our mood immediately, making us feel happy from the inside. There were moments where I literally used this in my healing with meditation and other relaxation techniques to help me put one foot in front of the other to survive each day.

Gratitude is not just having your mind on where you want to go and being glad that you're not where you were—it's being grateful in the moment for where you are right now, as imperfect and unfinished as it is. Because gratitude lets you open up compassion for yourself. When you open compassion for yourself, you start gaining resilience.

A study published in *Behavior Research and Therapy*_found that Vietnam War veterans with higher levels of gratitude experienced lower rates of post-traumatic stress disorder.[1] Another study published in the *Journal of Personality and Social Psychology* found that gratitude was a major contributor to resilience following the terrorist attacks on September 11.[2] Gratitude also increases self-esteem, reduces depression, and boosts immunity.

If you look for things you can be thankful for every day, you'll also boost your mental muscle. It's essential to make it a habit to think about what you appreciate. Find those moments in a day when you acknowledge gratitude.

Sometimes I stop in the middle of what I'm doing to breathe in a moment of gratitude. Again, it's sort of like stopping to smell the flowers. It gives me a sense of satisfaction and new energy.

---

1. Kashdan, Todd B., Gitendra Uswatte, Terri Julian 2006. "Gratitude and hedonic and eudaimonic well-being in Vietnam war veterans. ScienceDirect." Behavior Research and Therapy 177-199. https://www.sciencedirect.com/science/article/abs/pii/S0005796705000392.
2. Morin, Amy 2015. "7 Scientifically Proven Benefits of Gratitude," Psychology Today. https://www.psychologytoday.com/us/blog/what-mentally-strong-people-dont-do/201504/7-scientifically-proven-benefits-gratitude.

I have an app on my Apple watch that buzzes at certain times of the day and takes me through breathing exercises for one minute. Another great way to build gratitude into your life is to make it a habit to think about what you're grateful for before getting out of bed in the morning or before going to sleep. Finding the silver lining shapes how we think about the world.

Strengthen Your Resilience with Gratitude

Gratitude is so powerful! It can change the way you see everything in your life and pull you right out of a spiral. It can improve your mental and physical health. Health experts believe that practicing gratitude has a physiological effect on your brain.

You will feel this effect in your spirit too. Gratitude allows you to weather the storms in a different way. When you look for things to be thankful for, you're putting on a pair of rose-colored glasses that make everything look brighter and sunnier.

Studies show that by focusing on the positive and feeling grateful, you can improve your sleep quality and reduce anxiety and depression. Without all the stress and crappy thoughts running through your mind, your body has fewer chances to produce stress hormones like cortisol that beat you up. Being thankful is linked to better moods, less fatigue, and less inflammation. All of these factors together reduce your risk of heart failure—and that's no small accomplishment! By being thankful, you can get your mind *and* your body right. You can live longer! Your health increases the resilience of your body, and gratitude increases the strength of your spirit.

Gratitude is taking a look around and being thankful for something. You can be grateful for the big things: big paychecks, big milestones, big anything. But when you can be grateful for every-thing—good and bad, big and small—you will strengthen your resilience. Gratitude is focusing on and appreciating what you have instead of dwelling on what you've lost, want, or don't have.

Gratitude helps you move along your journey, in a way that enables resilience. The *International Journal of Social Psychiatry* published a study that found a strong positive correlation between gratitude, resilience, and feelings of happiness. [3] It showed that participants who felt more grateful and practiced gratitude journ-aling were found happier and emotionally stronger than others. On depressive patients, it showed that those who practiced gratitude exercises recovered soon and felt more motivated to bounce back from their distress. Everybody has a journey. That journey is full of things that will test your resilience: trauma, obstacles, aging, milestones—you name it. And when you encounter these things on your journey, you either stop short or keep going. A daily practice of gratitude will give you the strength to keep going.

Gratitude is powerful because it helps you see your journey in a whole different way, and that will push you to do more. Obstacles aren't as intimidating when you can look at the sky and focus on how beautiful the journey is.

Gratitude is the opposite of resentment or bitterness—it's about being flexible. It gives you the power to see ways to jump, slide, and move through anything that comes your way. If you're stuck in bitterness, which is very inflexible, you can never have resilience. You'll be too locked into the past to see all the good things going on in the present!

3. Chowdhury, Madhuleena Roy 2022. "The Neuroscience of Gratitude and How It Affects Anxiety & Grief," Positive Psychology. https://positivepsychology. com/neuroscience-of-gratitude/.

When you're grateful, you see opportunities you can take on right now! I saw the blue sky above me and a life filled with possibilities ahead of me when I first came to California and started practicing gratitude. Everything looked clearer! Every day was a chance to be positive and say "thank you." The clouds lifted, and I saw my next steps, all because I was grateful!

Here's how I practice gratitude. I find the smallest things that can bring me a little joy, and I zone in on them. Try this with me right now. Look around. When I look around, I see a beautiful flower in front of me. I'm grateful for that.

I see the tea next to me on my desk. I'm grateful for that. What do you see? Say it out loud! Feel, smell, or taste it. Saturate yourself in the glory of that moment.

The rest of my day might be a pile of crap, but those two things are really wonderful. That's what will keep me going. No matter where you are or what's going on, you can practice gratitude.

Be grateful for the detours in your life because they show you things you wouldn't have otherwise seen on your journey.

To start practicing gratitude, you have to shift your mindset away from the Jones Principle. You've heard the saying "keeping up with the Joneses"? Well, too often, we focus on who is doing better than we are; then, we think about all the things we don't have instead of appreciating what we do have.

One of my clients was a distraught woman who told me all the things she disliked about herself and the things she wanted and didn't have. So many people fall into that habit. I used to do that to myself too until I recognized how bad it was making me feel and how it affected my life overall. The healing benefits of gratitude changed everything for me.

When you find that happening, divert your attention and get rid of the Jones Principle. Bring your thoughts to your own backyard and use the Gratitude Principle instead.

Focus your attention away from other people and what they are doing and look within. Think to yourself, "Right now is good. Things could have been worse." This might feel weird at first because you've become accustomed to the habit of comparing yourself to others. Hang in there, and it will get better. Promise!

At first, you might have to force-feed yourself positive chatter by repeating quotes and affirmations night and day. After a while, you believe what you're telling yourself. With practice, you are more likely to get back on your feet and see the light at the end of the tunnel because you're looking for it and not distracted by what everyone else has going on in their lives.

Strengthen Your Resilience with Self-Awareness

When was the last time you just gave yourself a moment to take in what's around you? I'm talking about everything: the past, the present, the feelings, the thoughts, the people—the big picture. The more you are aware of the bigger picture, the more you learn about the choices you've made and what to do to make good choices and great decisions in the future.

To shift your mind to the Gratitude Principle and see the positive things surrounding you, you have to pause. Stop, take a breath, and become aware of everything that's around you, good and bad. Awareness prevents you from repeating history or falling into old patterns. Gratitude expands your awareness, and with awareness, you can strengthen your resilience!

41

Know that you can be better. Consciously tell yourself that until you believe it! And know this is something you have to practice *every day.*

So, where do you start? How can you begin to become self-aware?

I always start by asking myself a few questions:

What am I feeling?

Why am I feeling that?

What did I think of that caused these feelings?

These questions aren't always easy to answer. Let's say you were having a good day until your mood tanked. So, you know your mood changed . . . but why? Let's say you smelled perfume at the doctor's office that reminded you of an aunt who was never nice to you. Now, you didn't see the aunt at the doctor's office. You weren't even thinking about the aunt, but that smell took you to that place you don't like to go.

Dig deeper. Ask yourself, "Why does thinking of that person make me feel bad? What happened there?" When you ask yourself these questions, you can find a lot of trauma, grief, or events you might not have thought about before, even though they affected you. Especially when things happen to us as children, we don't allow ourselves to feel those feelings. We push them aside. We make so many excuses for adults who hurt us! Even if we know how a person or event affected us, we deny what our awareness brings up.

When you dig deep and are honest with yourself about the impact of these people or events, you can start to heal. And you have to realize that you're not being disloyal to the person when you recognize that they made a mistake or didn't treat you right. All adults screw up. By seeing their faults, however, you take the blame off yourself and start to move forward.

This process may seem difficult at first, but micro gratitude steps will take you a long way! We are often resistant to labeling these uncomfortable feelings because we don't want to admit that our loved ones hurt us. But when you recognize that this human being screwed up and you paid the price for it, you can put things into a more honest perspective. Don't feel guilty about that. Be self-aware, answer the "why," solve it, and resolve to move on without guilt and angst.

As you age, you have to continue these practices and become aware of being in your physical body. Our bodies change! The things that might have served you well in the past may not continue to be best for you as your body enters menopause or andropause. When you notice this happening, it's time to make changes!

In the past, I dealt with trauma and loss by punishing myself. I didn't eat, didn't drink water, didn't do the things that are nourishing and good for my body. That self-punishment came from a negative place. I told myself I wanted to honor a person I had lost, but I actually didn't feel like I deserved happiness or strength or any of the things I do deserve.

As I became more aware of this, I started making different choices. Whenever I catch myself drifting toward that self-punishment place, I choose to do the opposite. I grab my water. I have a meal. I intentionally do something comforting and nourishing. Because of that, I'm okay with myself and do things that make me feel better down the line.

Even as I make those choices, I stay aware of what's going on. My body used to shut down when I faced shock and loss. Even my taste buds would shut down! So, when I consciously choose to eat a meal and make myself feel better, I make sure I am aware of every bite. I eat very slowly, feeling the nutrition and reminding myself of the goodness I'm eating.

Sometimes, I meditate to help enhance my state of consciousness. Other times, I watch a movie intently to take myself away from my thoughts and give myself a break. It all depends on what I need at the time.

Practicing awareness can help you tap into the things that will nourish and fuel you. That strengthens your resilience and gives you the ability to get back up after you've been knocked down. I can get back up more easily when I'm well-fed and hydrated, right? That all starts with self-awareness.

Strengthen Your Resilience with Self-Care

Some people live very much in their minds and ignore their bodies. Others live through their physicality and don't spend as much time in their head. Part of self-awareness is bringing back that balance between mind and body through gratitude and self-care. These all work together to help strengthen your resilience!

Gratitude is mental self-care, but don't forget about physical self-care! Taking care of body and mind isn't natural for everyone. We focus so much of our time on caring for our children and loved ones that we forget about ourselves. Don't forget about you!

It's time to embrace the importance of taking care of yourself. If you neglect yourself, you can't go far, and you won't feel like doing anything, either. If you neglect yourself, you risk having a shorter life and more problems with your health.

We all know someone who just can't seem to treat themselves with the same kindness they show to other people. Maybe that person is you. If you're one of those people, use the awareness tool I just talked about, and go inward. Make a regular habit of thinking about things that will make you feel good. It's time for you to put your feet up, run a bubble bath, or do whatever you need to do to relax your body and mind. A nice therapeutic bath sounds so good to me right now. Try it! You might just like it!

Think about what you would do for someone else if they felt the way you do when you're broken or in a bad place. Pretend you're with a best friend or a loved one. How would you try to take care of them to make them feel better? Would you cook their favorite meal? Encourage them to go to bed early? Watch their favorite movie with them? Now turn that caring inward for yourself.

All those things you would do for somebody else, you can and should offer to yourself.

Self-care comes in so many forms! Eating healthy, drinking water, planning fun activities and distractions, spending time at the spa, meditating, shopping, reading, and more! Go out there and do that for yourself, and don't feel guilty! There are psychological benefits that you can gain from watching a favorite movie or rereading your favorite book when you're stressed. When you pick up something you've already seen before, you already know how it ends. You can enjoy the journey with no anxiety or anticipation. There is a reason we go back and watch our favorite shows when we're having a difficult day—it actually does help!

Strengthen Your Resilience with Purpose

Self-care extends your life. Self-awareness extends your life. Gratitude extends your life. Purpose gives you the *drive* to extend your life. It gives you energy. Purpose makes life exciting and meaningful. If you have a clear idea of what you're striving for and why, you are much more likely to stay strong when things get tough.

Purpose will wake you in the morning in a good mood and have you working through your day with intention and strategy, which can make anybody's day fulfilling.

We're put here on different journeys to change the world. It's up to each of us to find our purpose. When I found my purpose and started my new life as a forty-three-year-old late bloomer, I had doubts. I regretted some things and faulted myself for my decisions. Why didn't I leave sooner? Why didn't I start training and get into the "people business" sooner? I had to get past those regrets by realizing that I made the best decisions I could with the knowledge and abilities I had right then. Would you fault a two-year-old for coloring outside the lines? Of course not. You don't know what you don't know when you're that young and immature. But at each stage of your life, you learn and grow. Apply that same reasoning to yourself when you think about past actions. When thoughts of self-blame pop up, cast them out! I began enjoying my life much more and felt less stressed when I looked past those regrets.

Some people start on their journeys early. Michael Jackson, for example, changed the world with his music when he was young. I started much later. My journey isn't Michael's, and yours isn't either! But you can start *today* if you haven't already. It's not too late. Now is exactly when you're meant to start.

This is an essential part of gaining resilience and can be accomplished easily. To find your purpose, start by talking to people. Strike up conversations with the people you meet and listen to stories about how they and others found their purpose. Explore your interests and what you love doing to prompt creative ideas. Think about what you loved to do as a child and revisit those things. Sit with yourself and do a self-assessment. Ask more questions:

What motivates you?

What matters most to you?

When are you the happiest?

If you make a habit of searching inward for your purpose through practices like meditation or other self-awareness methods, you will eventually land on that thing that creates purpose in your life, lights your fire, and has you wanting more!

Micro Moves to Cultivate Gratitude and Strengthen Resilience

Each of us holds the power to maintain a rich, powerful, and resilient life! You just have to develop the habits and skills for that to shine through. At the center of those habits are practices for cultivating gratitude. And just like with resilience, gratitude starts with itty-bitty steps. Think *micro gratitude*.

Micro gratitude could be a situation where you realize that your life is a dumpster fire. Pause. Assess. You can still ask yourself, "What am I grateful for in this very minute?"

- Well, you may not be in pain. That's something to be grateful for!

- You may not be sick. That's definitely something to be grateful for!

- Do you know that you'll have dinner or a safe place to sleep?

We take a lot of those things for granted when we're not in a gracious state of mind. And yet, many people can't count on having safety, security, or food. You might not have these things tomorrow, the next day, or a year from now, but right now, things are all right. You have a whole list of things to be grateful for if you just take a moment to stop and think.

I'm grateful I had time to talk to my sister, kids, niece, and grandkids today. It's the little things that really matter. This exercise will get you through the tough times! To help you on your gratitude journey, here are a few micro moves that will help you see the good things even in bad times:

- Appreciate everything: the good, the bad, and the ugly. It's all part of your journey for a reason!

- Practice mindfulness. Meditate, do yoga, or just sit with yourself.

- Keep a gratitude journal.

- Volunteer. This is a wonderful way to find your purpose!

- Express yourself and express gratitude to others.

- Spend time with loved ones.

- Improve your happiness in other areas of your life

Today, I am so grateful that I get to wake up in a cozy bed, make a cup of tea, and help people find their purpose at all ages. What a great feeling! When people ask, "Wendy, how did you make it? How did you push through? How did you release your heart to love again, laugh again, and win competitions?" I tell them that this journey starts with gratitude. It can get you out of any rut, any slump, and improve your life. Gratitude helped me to survive.

Some of the following micro gratitude moves will help you gain resilience. These micro moves are easy to do, they require little time. You can do them anywhere—even in your own backyard—and they don't cost a thing!

List What You're Grateful For:

◆ Stop and step outside of yourself. Take a look at the world around you to see nature and the beauty it holds. For example: Find one flower and think about the beauty it adds to the universe, watch a squirrel or a bird, watch the wind in the trees, look at the moon. It will put things in perspective and diminish what you once thought was a big problem. It will reduce your stress, and your problem may feel more manageable.

◆ Rewatch a favorite show, and be thankful for the talent of the people who created it for you to enjoy.

◆ Eat a ripe piece of fruit, and be thankful with each bite for the taste and texture, the hands that picked it, and the land that nurtured it.

◆ Before preparing food, be grateful for the people involved in every step of getting it from farm to table.

◆ Pet your dog, your cat, or whatever animal you are near to appreciate the comfort and unconditional love it provides, or watch someone else's animal from afar. If you don't have an animal you can connect with, appreciate the animals on social media and find humor in things they do.

◆ Look at a painting in an online museum that speaks to you and be grateful for the beauty and talent.

◆ Stop when you're reading a good book to be grateful to the author who envisioned the story and shared it with you.

◆ Be grateful for your cozy blanket, comfy slippers, or favorite mug and appreciate the comfort it gives you in that moment.

Create an Environment in Your Home That Encourages and Uplifts You to Help Keep You Strong

I hang pictures with positive messages where I will see them often, and I play happy or relaxing music that puts me in a good mood. I surround myself with happy memories.

Reframe Annoyances into Gratitude

◆ Instead of being annoyed at trying to fit another leftover into the fridge, be grateful that you are blessed to have so much food.

◆ Sick of cleaning? Take a moment to think about being grateful for your apartment or house.

◆ Annoyed at kids/pets? Be thankful they are healthy and are an active part of your life.

Tell Someone How Much You Appreciate Them

◆ Praise the positive—even if you feel it's someone's job to do a certain thing, let them know you are grateful anyway. For example, thank a child for making their bed or feeding the dog. Thank your partner for washing the dishes or taking out the garbage. Everyone benefits from this. It makes others feel appreciated. It makes you feel good, and it becomes a reciprocal cycle.

◆ Quit worrying about the big picture stuff you can't change, and find something small and beautiful to focus on. Sometimes the grand scheme of things can get you down.

Avoid Negativity that Distracts from Gratitude

- ◆ Spend less time with negative friends or family members.
- ◆ Be aware of media toxicity and social media trolls.

I do these things, and they soothe my soul every time. Think of it this way—you're looking through a camera lens at a close-up of someone (maybe it's you) who is having a bad day. When you shift your mental focus to being grateful for the beauty of things outside of you, the camera lens widens to include all of those beautiful things in your life and spirit. When that happens, it feels like warm and fuzzy sunshine. It makes you feel better and will let you reframe whatever you were experiencing; it will remind you that it's not that serious.

PART TWO

Rebuild

WENDY'S WISDOM:

Change and comfort can't exist in the same space.

CHAPTER 4

The Hallway

"Our dilemma is that we hate change and love it at the same time;
what we really want is for things to remain the same but get better."

—Sydney J. Harris

After I settled down in my new home with my sister Sylvia and her family, I had no idea that the real work was ahead. My life up to that point was a whirlwind of pain, suffering, and survival—an out-of-body experience. I thought I would never find my way out of that bad place and be able to move toward achieving the goals and dreams I had for myself as a little girl.

So many things in life can throw us off track and threaten to derail us, jeopardizing our longevity and happiness. Our physical, mental and emotional health is always at risk if we do not stay aware of what's happening in the world and within us as we go through life experiences.

Here's what I found when I was finally focused on my own body. More pain. More suffering. I still felt trapped, even though I was free. Changing my life and arriving in safety thrust my body into what I call "the Hallway." Some of the toughest times in my life were when I was in the in-between space bridging where

I'd been and my future. That's why I think of it as a Hallway—because it wasn't a destination; it was a place I had to walk through to get from one place to another.

What I didn't know at the time was that a new challenge awaited me in the Hallway—dealing with the emotions I hadn't been able to process while my physical body was in danger. I was running on pure adrenaline when I was escaping my abuser—and when I was finally free, the other emotions came flooding in.

I remember two women asking, "Wendy, how did you do it? How did you make it through the transition from abuse to safety? From divorce to trusting someone again?" They asked me this because they want these things for themselves too. And guess what? They can have it. You can do it too! The Hallway is an important piece to the puzzle.

But first, let's talk more about what the Hallway is.

What Is the Hallway?

Three things remain constant in this life—death, taxes, and change. Life continually changes as we embark on many roads to find our ultimate paths. Change is what the Hallway is all about.

The Hallway is an emotional throughway not a destination. The Hallway is a processing ground for the emotions evoked by new life changes. You enter a Hallway when a change comes into your life, and you leave it when you've weathered the transition and processed the emotions brought up by the change.

The Hallway is that space between where life gets interrupted from its normal pattern by a different, unusual, or unexpected major change and the recovery, adjustment and/or acceptance to that shift. It's a process that enables you to adjust before you can fully embrace a new way of being.

THE HALLWAY

Hallways are a natural part of life just like hunger, fatigue, and recovering from illness, injury, or hard work because life changes occur all the time—good changes, bad changes, unexpected and uninvited changes.

Navigating change is tough at any level, and the more dramatic your shift, the more challenging the transition is likely to feel. It's the space in which you grieve what you need to let go of to be able to accept what is coming your way. As with grief, the Hallway has many phases, and it takes mindfulness to get through it.

Whether your change is big or small, sad or happy—like a promotion, marriage, new baby, new business—adjusting is always a difficult phase that causes stress and discomfort.

Even small changes can be vexing, like updating your phone and discovering that everything works differently. All the things you could do without thinking now require extra attention until you've learned the new system. The transition period is annoying no matter how much you might like your phone's new features. Your old phone might have been slow and out of date and hard to fix, but it was familiar.

Then gradually, you get the hang of the new phone, and you start to appreciate the features. Leaving the old model behind isn't difficult anymore, and you might wonder why you ever hesitated in the first place.

In the Hallway, we journey from the familiar to the unknown. The unknown is always scary. Even if the familiar was bad or dangerous, when we're uncomfortable with change we tend to tell ourselves that it wasn't that bad (it was). But when you work through the discomfort of dealing with what's unfamiliar, eventually you discover that what lies ahead is so much better than what you left behind.

The bigger and more uncomfortable the change—like moving out of state, getting married, love relationship breakups, family drama, financial woes, or becoming an empty nester—the larger the impact. So, they take longer to process as we move through the Hallway.

The changes that really impact us, however, are the ones we don't see coming—like the unexpected loss of a job or relationship, an injury, death, or a devastating medical diagnosis.

Sometimes more than one change comes along while you're in the Hallway. Don't be surprised to find that the Hallway "magically" lengthens when that happens. You thought you were almost to the other end, and now it's stretched out again. That's because you have more processing to do with this new change.

When life piles up on the changes, processing takes longer. Not only that, but multiple significant changes can drain your energy and spirit. That makes the Hallway seem even longer and darker. Your confidence dims, and you're unsure how to deal with everything at once.

I found myself in a triple whammy Hallway after I left New Jersey with multiple, simultaneous life changes to process. My children and I had relocated across the country. We were processing the separation from my ex-husband. Suddenly I was single for the first time in many years and head of the household. I had to work through emotions I had been running from for years.

But even though I was afraid when faced with adjusting to these new situations, I didn't let fear paralyze me. I pushed on and faced my demons head-on every step of the way.

This is something I preach to my clients all the time. It's okay to feel afraid while you are moving on to new territory or making adjustments in life. Anything new and different is scary. Everybody feels afraid sometimes, from the person who lives on the street to the president of the United States.

How Do You End Up in the Hallway?

When I started to understand what it meant to be in the Hallway, I realized that this process would happen over and over because everything in life changes all the time.

You will experience more changes than you can count in your lifetime. You'll move several times! You'll change relationships and change jobs. You'll be separated from your family at some point. Life is a constant adjustment of holding on and letting go. Living means growing, moving, and transforming.

Sometimes you think you know where the Hallway is going, especially when the change you've made is positive and voluntary. But the way can seem dark and scary when you didn't choose the shift. You may not be able to imagine what lies ahead or that it could possibly be good—maybe even better than anything you've had before.

Don't panic. There is always a way out of the Hallway. Even though change is good and is meant to help us grow, it often derails us. If we don't learn to process change in a healthy way, it can throw us off track and stop us from achieving our life goals and deepest dreams. Unhealthy responses to change can ruin our health and sap our resilience.

Think about a Hallway that you've been in during your life. You may even be in one now. Everything is going great, and then something unexpected happens, and the shock derails you—changes how you feel, think, and react. You might feel like you're in a tailspin, making your way through a dark tunnel. Fear takes over. Now you've been thrown into the Hallway, and it's time to start processing. Start by observing how you feel and what actions you are taking out of habit or panic.

Maybe you think that nothing else matters because you're so overwhelmed by darkness. You neglect yourself because you can't see how important your body and health are. Instead, all you can focus on is the grief, stress, or discomfort of the change that just occurred.

Change affects our mental, emotional, and physical health. Successfully navigating the Hallway requires sifting through emotions and physical reactions to adapt. When you find yourself feeling overwhelmed, it means you're in the middle of the Hallway—and possibly dealing with more than one change.

Getting through the Hallway isn't as easy as just plowing forward. Additional changes may mean you need to back up and retrace your path. Maybe so much happens at once that you feel all turned around. Sometimes you might be so tired you don't think you can take another step. When that happens, remember that making your way through the Hallway is a process—and it requires patience.

Who Do Hallways Happen to and Why?

Hallways happen to everyone, but they can look vastly different as you age. Young people move through Hallways easier. Within five years, a young person may have changed schools, jobs, or partners without blinking an eye. As you get older, you settle into a routine, you have more responsibilities, and more is at stake, so the changes you experience can rock your world and have a greater impact on your health. From my personal experience, the changes I go through today hit me differently than they did thirty or forty years ago.

Women go through menopause which is a unique journey in itself. Our hormones force us to encounter change in different ways. Hot flashes, mood swings, night sweats, and more change our bodies, minds, and schedules, making it exceedingly difficult to manage. Men go through it too—their "change of life" as they age is called andropause. This massive shift in our bodies is definitely a Hallway to be navigated.

As we age, we might find ourselves dealing more frequently with grief. Our parents pass away. Our brothers, sisters, friends, and colleagues eventually die. We have to reckon with knowing that the people we're losing may be our age—we can't tell ourselves anymore that only "old" people die. COVID alone has taken so many people away from us before their time. People we've known for decades will suddenly not be a part of our lives anymore. And although death, taxes, and change are the only constants in our lives, that doesn't mean these things don't affect us mentally and physically.

On *top* of all that, we grapple with the inevitable. We start to fear what is ahead. We start to think about how much time we have left, or what we haven't been able to do, or what abilities we're losing. Don't go there! Put those energies into those you love (including yourself) and the joys you can experience here and now. You have to stay positive to keep moving forward.

Studies have shown that people who focus on the darkness, who think about how little time they have left, are more likely to leave this earth sooner. What we focus on determines the direction we're going. Find meaning in your life to get you through the tough times in the Hallway, and it will extend your life.

That reminds me of a video I will never forget.

A ninety-six-year-old woman married a ninety-five-year-old man. Their optimism in marrying at their age struck me, as well as their love for each other. They literally thrived on each other's energy.

The video started out with how this man was taking care of his wife by showing her how to stay active by doing an exercise routine with her. Later, I saw how they would lie in bed talking and sharing or sit in their rockers having cute conversations. She was clearly his reason for living. You could see it gave him joy. She represented life for him and something to strive for and he represented unconditional love and security for her.

The families didn't support their marriage, however, so they separated the two by relocating the man's wife to live with a relative in another state. As a result, the husband collapsed and succumbed to death shortly afterward. Without his wife he had no reason to live. I'm fairly sure that he had what they call broken heart syndrome.

The University of Birmingham immunologists claim that an increase in stress hormones can make people sick with grief, and this emotionally driven sickness can get worse the older you are. So, there's no doubt in my mind that this man's stress increased greatly and as a result caused heart issues. This man was in the last Hallway of his life because he no longer had purpose.

Surviving the Hallway is a balancing act and along with purpose, self-care is a primary concern. Caring for the body, getting proper rest, giving yourself mental breaks, eating well or creating joyful moments along the way are even more important when you're in the Hallway.

Our bodies react to change in peculiar ways, and that reaction will vary depending on whether you're twenty, thirty, fifty, or seventy. Every change you make will test your resiliency. The older you get, the more you have to rethink, redefine, and reinvent your approach to new and even familiar situations to create the foundation for strength and resiliency.

Managing the Hallway

Have you ever wondered why some people give up and stop short of their dreams while others achieve great personal successes over and over again throughout their lifetime? The difference is how they manage their Hallways of change.

Here's what I know: Time heals, but you can't just sit back and wait for healing to happen on its own. You've got to be proactive not reactive or you can get stuck in the Hallway. You can literally die in the Hallway if you wait for the passage of time to solve things.

What you do while waiting for time to heal is crucial. How are you going to deal with your physical, emotional, and mental state while time passes? The choices you make in the hallway have a significant impact on how you'll emerge from the Hallway. Your decisions determine whether you'll come out healthy and strong or angry and bitter.

In the Hallway, you confront pain, disappointment, shame, and grief. You learn and have to accept hard truths. If more than one circumstance has sent you into the Hallway, you're likely to have those complicated emotions about each situation. And if those events are interconnected (as they often are), there can be a lot of going forward and backward or in circles before you get to the end.

Healing takes time. Just like mending a broken bone or having a baby, it can't be rushed or skimped on if you want a good outcome. You can't just run down the clock because how long it takes is different for everyone. That's why it's so important to have a plan and an intention about how you will make it through the Hallway. It's not enough just to survive—you need to prepare to thrive.

So how do you process the Hallway when trauma or grief shut down parts of the brain? How do you create a mindset to see the possibilities? How do you find the light to see the doorways to get out of the Hallway?

Whenever I have gone through change, I know the kind of thoughts that went through my mind. I knew I had to heal, but it was difficult to concentrate when I was hurting so bad. I didn't know when the pain would end, and I wondered if it would ever go away completely. I worried that the feelings might be with me forever, popping back up when I least expected. Life felt cruel and random. Hope began to fade.

Those feelings are all part of the transition that is the Hallway. You're between what was and what can be. What you process, hang onto, and let go of will all prepare you for creating your Life After. That's why it's so important to be aware of the Hallway and make choices instead of just drifting or waiting for time to magically solve the issues. If you depend on drifting or waiting to create your future, you might not be happy with where you end up.

When you drift and wait, you give up control. You tell the universe that you'll settle for anything. This is the biggest factor that sabotages people's efforts to make positive changes, whether those shifts involve self-care, career choices, or relationships.

Unless you know what's happening to you while you're in the Hallway and find the courage to work through everything you are feeling, you can't move forward to enjoy a fulfilling life, good love relationship, successful career, or a healthy body.

This may not be your first journey through the Hallway if you've processed past losses. It's important to keep in mind that since each change is different from what happened before, it will process differently, and your responses will not be the same.

People think that I've never had issues just because I smile today. Well, they are wrong. I've had my share, and I can smile today because I did the work to heal. Even though I'll always be a work in progress the healing I have done has allowed me to move forward and to keep challenging myself repeatedly.

The critical question here is *how* you weather the storm or go the distance from the beginning of the Hallway to the end while waiting for time to heal. I have grappled with that often while in the Hallway. In fact, I happen to be in the Hallway as I write this.

My baby brother Scotty recently passed away. He had a massive heart attack only a few days after his fifty-third birthday. I feel the emotions—a little selfish, angry, sad—but also glad he's not in pain. I have to sit back and breathe, count my blessings, and think about the times I did have with him. It's so difficult to do that. If you've experienced a death, you know what I mean.

He was such a loving, kind, and innocent spirit who saw life through the eyes of a child, but he was also responsible and dedicated to his family. I have to quiet the voice in my head that plays over and over with "woulda, coulda, shoulda"—things I wish I had done differently. Even though I'm grieving, I still find ways to lift my spirits; I use my meditation time to help quiet my mind and strengthen my faith.

This time around, I have paid close attention to taking care of myself. I feel gratitude that I am still here to continue my journey and fight for what is right for myself and my brother. I am also grateful that I still have loving family and friends. Sometimes the pain seeps through at unexpected times and distracts me. And I feel selfish and wish for him to be with me again. When that happens, I pray, focus, and meditate again. Then I laugh about the good times. There is always something you can find to laugh about—a funny picture, a good joke, a silly song or video, or a comedy on TV. In my case, I can also listen to the music my brother mixed (which includes his voice) right before his death. They called him DJ Milk.

It's okay to laugh while you grieve. It's okay to laugh and cry at the same time. Laughter is healing. Laughing when you are dealing with pain isn't inappropriate or disrespectful. It's part of healing, just like eating and sleeping. Laughing heals the heart and helps you reconnect to living. Don't let anyone shame you for taking this key step.

Sometimes, you'll feel an emotional whiplash going from being sad to finding something funny. You might go through several cycles in a row, like waves coming in and going out—sad/funny. It can feel confusing, but it's normal and natural. Those sparks of joy strengthen your sanity and endurance. When you practice seizing that joy, you start to notice more opportunities to do so, and the joyful times get stronger and longer within your soul.

At night when I hit a rough spot, I console myself and ask God for the strength to endure the grief and pain while I'm waiting for healing to happen.

My daily positive habits ensure that I won't sacrifice my health again while I'm grieving. My brother wouldn't want that either. Being self-defeating is a thing of the past for me. Once my therapist made me aware of how I used to punish myself by not taking care of my body when I was in a tough spot—in the Hallway—I'm now super-aware of my choices. Making good choices gives me back some control. I'm not tossed about at the mercy of the storm. It's a new way of being and doing when these things happen to me now.

Life never stops handing you changes, but how you respond affects how you will move forward and grow in life.

According to psychologists, there are stages and phases you have to process through before you can overcome any form of grief. To make it out of the Hallway in a healthy way, you can't skip any of the stages or hurry the process.

The Doors in the Hallway

There are seven doors in the Hallway. Each one leads to a different stage of your healing. They each represent a phase and the feeling you have to process to heal. When you process that feeling, it unlocks each door and you can make your way through to the end of the hallway.

The Seven Doors to Healing Are:

- ◆ **Door #1 Disbelief**—At the first sign of change you are automatically thrust into the Hallway, and through that first door. What smacks you right in the face is disbelief. You're numb. Your mind freezes, and the clock stops.

- ◆ **Door #2 Disown/Disavow**—Things are still new at this point and as you grapple with the reality of your situation, it doesn't make sense. So, you fool yourself into thinking it doesn't really exist. You temporarily disconnect and disavow every detail about it. You literally check out!

To unlock this door—talk things through with someone to face the reality of your new situation.

- **Door #3 Guilt/Regret**—In this stage, people tend to beat themselves up. You dwell on things you did or didn't do. You ask a lot of "what ifs" to yourself. What if I had gotten there sooner? Or you might have the "woulda, coulda, shoulda" syndrome. If I would've only paid more attention to him . . . I could've been a better mom, dad, or friend . . . I should've called and said I love you. *To unlock this door*—acknowledge the guilt. Talk about it with others. Journal your regrets. Write a letter of apology if you feel responsible, and then forgive yourself and let it go.

- **Door #4 Outrage/Negotiation**—After you settle down and reality sets in, you begin to feel the pain of your new situation. You want to resist and change what has happened. You can become frustrated and may even lash out. Bartering or negotiating with a higher power is common. *To unlock this door*—Express your feelings and talk about all the things you are furious about. Go for a walk, tire yourself out with a workout, sign up for therapy, or go to the gym and wallop a punching bag.

- **Door #5: Sadness/Despair**—This is probably the most difficult stage. When you understand the gravity of how the change in your life affects you, your spirit takes a dive. Sadness, despair, and feelings of helplessness take hold, and it becomes a very painful cycle of uncertainty and fear. Loneliness, sleeplessness, appetite changes, and isolation are common. *To unlock this door*—vocalize your emotions while finding some logical and relatable resolve. Find guidance with a therapist, mentor, coach, spiritual counselor, confidant or someone you trust. Focus on a goal you are passionate about for redirection and meaning.

- ◆ **Door #6 Adapt/Accept**—This is the infant stage of coming to grips with the fact that you cannot change what's happened, so you've adapted (somewhat) to the situation and accepted it for what it is. When you do that, you are able to step outside of the Hallway and can move forward. *To unlock this door*—create a new meaning for your life. Take ownership of yourself and your actions, while you continue work toward changing your behavior as it relates to others.

- ◆ **Door #7 Embrace and Prepare to Return to the Hallway**—This is the reconstruction phase. At this point, you are outside of the Hallway, but you still have to make way for your emotions to mature so you can reconstruct your life and emotions to handle the Hallway when it comes around again. *To unlock this door*—get clear on the fact that change is an endless process and must be embraced. Embracing the change will help you grow and prepare you for the next Hallway with strength, wisdom, and experience.

The key to successfully navigating the Hallway and finding happiness on the other end is to identify what you're feeling and allow yourself to process the emotions.

Sometimes we refuse to name what we're feeling because someone taught us that certain emotions are bad. Maybe you were told that being angry is a sin or that it's wrong to be angry. That's not true. Anger is a normal reaction when you feel like something has been taken from you or you've been treated unfairly. It's okay to feel like that, but what are you going to do about it? It's not a healthy response to punch someone, yell at people, or put your hand through the wall. Don't feel shame about how you feel and don't do anything because of those feelings that would cause you to be ashamed of your actions.

We take in so many toxic ideas from what our culture tells us or what people around us may have told us. They only repeat what someone incorrectly told them.

Maybe you were told that feeling sad or depressed is a weakness. That's not true either. Men worry that they might seem less masculine if they admit to feeling sad, but the truth is, we're all humans, and humans have feelings. It's okay to cry. Crying is one of the ways our body helps us release emotions. Holding everything inside can lead to other physical and mental problems. Let it out!

Don't let people rush you through the Hallway. Our culture isn't patient; it glorifies instant results even if they don't last. The people around you might push you to "get over it" because they are uncomfortable with your feelings. Maybe they were shamed for showing their own emotions, or they just don't know what to do. Don't listen to them. You've got to navigate the Hallway at your own speed.

Nobody can work through trauma or grief in a hurry. It's a personal experience, and each person has their own time frame to get through it. Just because someone else did it faster doesn't matter. You don't know if they were faking it or if the way they processed or didn't process their issues turned out to be positive and healthy. You can't compare your Hallway to anyone else's—and you can't compare your current Hallway to those you've traveled in the past.

I have tried to take the shortcut to skip these stages, and my plan failed every time. I was only fooling myself. Instead, I prolonged my misery by thinking I was okay. It takes a little courage to face your fear, but it's definitely doable and worth it in the end. I'm living proof of that, and with guided assurance, it's something that can help you grow. It's important to ask for help when you need it.

People heal after breaking a bone and being in a cast. They walk again or use their arms again, but it takes time. If they try to rush the healing, they make things worse and have to start all over again. Give yourself the time you need—and while you are healing, take control by finding ways to enhance and improve your physical and mental health. Once you deal with the feelings in the Hallway, you can learn to love and smile again, win your battles, and find your confidence once more.

It is essential that you work through each of the stages of grief to strengthen your resilience. That will help you find the keys to unlock the doors and get you out of the Hallway.

Let me repeat: Healing *is a natural process*, just like mending a broken bone or having a baby. It takes the time that it takes—and you can't speed that up!

Micro Moves to Get You through the Hallway

Do what I call your ABCs when you find yourself in the Hallway. It will help you throughout your journey.

- ◆ **Awareness:** Stop and assess what's going on at the initial onset of an occurrence. You can't fix anything unless you check out your environment and what you're experiencing. Live in the moment, and ask yourself how you are reacting and what you are feeling.

- ◆ **Breathe:** Practice rhythmic breathing methods. Inhale and exhale slowly while focusing on breath at the first signs of shock or change. At night when trying to sleep, breathe deeply and count backward starting at 300. Repeat as needed.

◆ **Care:** Eat and hydrate for better coping skills. Make appointments during your day to check in with yourself and assess. Maybe it's a good time for a healthy snack, a glass of water, a walk outside, or a short nap. Take a few minutes to text a supportive friend. Regular check-ins keep you from getting into a slump and help you maintain the energy and health you need to endure what you are going through. To power down to a deeper level, reduce anxiety and to restore patience, practice meditation techniques.

CHAPTER 5

A Dangerous Place to Get Stuck

"The changes we dread most may contain our salvation."

—Barbara Kingsolver

N avigating the Hallway is where most people sink or swim. The Hallway has some tough challenges, and the more you fight against that reality, the more painful it will be.

When I told you my real work began after I settled in California—it's the truth! After my great escape, I was not only thrown into the Hallway, but I got *stuck* in the Hallway. I fought, resisted, and went down kicking and screaming as I sank deeper and deeper into depression. I went from one Hallway to another trying to reclaim my life. I was glad, relieved, sad, afraid, and regretful. As I thought more about my experiences and walked further into the Hallway, I got angry. Oh, I was so angry! Angry about what he did to me, angry that I didn't stop the abuse sooner, angry that I couldn't take my rage out on him, angry because I was so ashamed. I was stuck in the Hallway and didn't know how to get out. That left me feeling broken for years.

What I didn't know was that my anger was a way to protect myself because underneath my rage, deep inside, I felt like a scared little animal trying to avoid destruction.

I had lived in fear for so long that I still felt like a victim imprisoned in my own mind. My spirit and confidence were stolen, and I felt it was too hard and too late to start over. I did nothing but sulk, cry, and feel sorry for myself, fearing someday I would be forced to go back to that miserable life.

I lashed out at everything during those first few years in the Hallway. I thought everyone was against me—people I knew and people I didn't know. Everything that could go wrong went wrong.

I'd go to the store to buy shoes, and I'd get home to find that the salesperson had put the wrong size in the bag. I'd order food and be served the wrong meal. Every darn thing was happening to me! And on a bad day, none of these moments feels small.

It wasn't just in my head either—other people in my family noticed it. They would ask, "Why does this stuff keep happening to you?" I believe my gloomy outlook created a feedback loop, and the universe reciprocated my negative energy.

That anger *and that fear* lasted for five years. I finally stepped out of that Hallway when I constructively confronted my emotions, saw them for what they really were, and worked through each stage of grief. In addition, therapy was a tremendous help. That's when my life completely changed.

Face Your Truth

The Hallway is exhausting and can encourage unhealthy responses to stress. It can wreak havoc on your relationships and stop your self-growth. It will reinforce negative or limiting beliefs about yourself. The Hallway will torment you if you stay too long.

The real problem with the emotions that come up while you're in the Hallway is that we have been trained to resist acknowledging or feeling them—or even admitting that they're real. We avoid them because they're uncomfortable. Society tells us not to be a downer. We feel like we're failing if we're not happy all the time—another lie our culture pushes. We even label feelings like anger and sadness as "negative" when they are actually normal and healthy.

Feeling emotions might not always be pleasant, but it's healthy. Do you know what's not healthy? Pretending that we feel nothing or becoming numb to the truth.

Sometimes we blow things up in our minds. We let worry get the best of us, and we start catastrophizing—thinking that the worst thing might actually happen. That makes every issue we deal with look like a big, hungry lion. When we step back, breathe, and use the gratitude principle, that big scary animal often turns out to be a little mouse in disguise.

Adjusting to change is a constant threat to our resilience. It is where people often get sidetracked or stuck in a vacuum of bitterness, trying to resist, stop, or reverse changes in their lives. That describes exactly where I was. *But don't go there!* Remember, changes are inevitable.

Trapped in a Dangerous Mental State

It's essential that you acknowledge your emotions and work through your feelings. Otherwise, you get paralyzed, and depression overrides every thought, and you make bad decisions. Then other things begin to fall apart. When you try to ignore your feelings, it affects your attitude, and negativity becomes a part of who you are. Negative energy feeds on more negative energy, and it spirals into self-sabotage. Don't let the Hallway trap you in this dangerous mental state!

By setting goals and taking micro steps, you can prevent yourself from getting stuck in the Hallway.

What you can do:

◆ Take stock of your situation. What landed you in the Hallway? Name the inciting incident. Was it a lost love, abuse, divorce, new job, or changes in your home/family?

◆ Don't ignore the small setbacks and frustrations. You'll need to deal with *all* the changes—small and large—that happen in the Hallway because they won't just go away, and leaving them unaddressed will hold you back.

◆ Dig deep to identify and face what you're feeling and everything that created the situation that put you in the Hallway. Then tackle those feelings and issues one at a time.

◆ Be honest with yourself.

Trapped in a Dangerous Physical State

Don't let tragedy, trauma, grief, stress, or anything in the Hallway become part of who you are. The longer you stay in the Hallway, the more you become a part of the Hallway (and the Hallway becomes a part of you).

Getting stuck in the Hallway can stop you from growing. Trauma and grief can manifest itself physically and rot you from the inside out. When those feelings and emotions are unprocessed and stuck in the body, you increase your risk of inflammation. Although inflammation can come to the rescue when you cut yourself or you hit your knee, it can worsen existing health problems *and* cause new ones when it's out of balance. Stress, trauma, and grief batter the immune system, leaving you depleted and discouraging you from activity. Over time, this can lead to increased blood pressure and the risk of blood clots.

When you get stuck anywhere—whether you are in the emotional Hallway of change, in a tunnel, or in an elevator—fear, panic and stress hormones will flood your body like a river and stun your muscles the same way broken heart syndrome does. So, not only will you experience physical symptoms like headaches, back pain, joint pain, or heart (chest) pains, but mentally you also will be operating at reduced capacity. If you feel sluggish, can't sleep or eat, or find that your memory is slipping—like forgetting to lock the door—that could be a stress reaction from being stuck in the Hallway affecting your brain.

Lingering life changes and prolonged stress in the Hallway will cause you to age faster, even if you are working out, eating right, and doing everything you can to stay healthy. I had a twenty-eight-year-old client graying right in front of my eyes because of the stress she endured while caring for her mother, who was painfully dying of pancreatic cancer over a two-year period.

It's important to move through the stages of grief as best you can. How long it takes to process grief is different with each loss and for every person.

Progress Can Zig-Zag

Psychologists say the grieving process can last anywhere from six months to four years on average (which means some people will go faster and others will move more slowly), and progress may show up in small ways. For example, you might sleep a little better one night, or it will be easier to get up in the morning, or you might have a bit more energy that day.

The key is to focus on self-care and moving through the stages of the Hallway. Progress isn't usually in a straight line. Shifting from one stage to another and cycling back around is normal. You may zig-zag or do spirals—what matters is that you are progressing. Give yourself permission to take "as long as it takes" to recover. Keep moving, don't get stuck, and remember that a little progress is still progress and that will keep you motivated to keep making progress.

Here's what being broken and stuck in a combination of Hallways was like for me. The Hallway I was stuck in was gradually closing in on me. The abuse I suffered was mental, emotional, physical, and sexual. Emotionally, I was having a hard time shaking it from my spirit. Nightmares had me screaming in the night. They still haunt me today. I felt like I was drowning. I thought I had no say about what happened to me, no options, no control, and no way out. I was desperate. I lost hope. I was on the edge of ending my life at one point. It's something I haven't talked about much because it makes me feel uncomfortable, because of the woman I am today, that it even entered my mind. Having said that, no one should ever feel ashamed or uncomfortable for reaching their limit. In fact, I wish the now-me could go back and embrace that frightened vulnerable me. Sometimes, there's a thin line between life and death or love and hate if you get stuck in the Hallway.

I also drank to numb myself. I just wanted the pain and fear to stop. I didn't want to be in my body anymore. I knew no other way to handle the trauma I was experiencing; I was in my early twenties with no reliable source of help to get me out. I had no mentor. I felt trapped and alone. I was thoroughly overwhelmed.

When we are in pain, we often forget to be kind to ourselves. Self-care and keeping our bodies strong take a back seat to more urgent priorities to deal with the situation causing our stress. That's why it's so important to stay on guard and remind ourselves that we are our greatest prize. Remember, awareness is the first step in the ABCs rule. We are worth taking care of, and self-care should be our highest priority.

Think of it this way: If your house isn't clean, you can't find what you need because of the clutter. If your body isn't healthy, you won't feel your best or think clearly. You're likely to spend more time than necessary in the Hallway, which can become a pattern of pain and suffering.

If you don't take care of yourself, you will get stuck in the Hallway. Taking care includes processing your feelings. Since we experience many confusing emotions in the Hallway, it's important to reach out for support to learn healthy coping skills and learn from the experience of others.

F.E.A.R.

FEAR is a huge reason people get stuck in the Hallway over and over again. It's an overwhelming emotion that creates a lot of imaginary obstacles, and these obstacles often feel life-threatening. Fear fools us into thinking that the thing that frightens us is insurmountable.

Getting stuck in your fears will crush dreams, ruin lives, and stop resilience in its tracks if you let it. When you push through the anxiety and fear, you can unlock every door in the Hallway, and you get better at it once you understand it.

In the movie *Star Wars*, Yoda warned Luke that fear, anger, and hatred lead to destruction and suffering. That is also true in real life!

Some people freeze in fear like a deer in the headlights. *But for me*, fear has two meanings:

Forget Everything And Run

or

Face Everything And Rise

When faced with fears, I challenge you to Face Everything And Rise!

Here are some ways you can do that:

a. Take a deep breath and closely examine what you're afraid of in the daylight.

b. Identify and work through your emotions.

c. Determine why this fear has a grip on you. If it's not life-threatening, take the risk. Do it. Push through it. Push past the fear by focusing on the good that will come from it and find the possibilities for yourself, your career, love relationships, health, or financial rewards. Get creative! Go over, under, around or through your obstacles to get to the other side.

d. Feel the gratitude within those possibilities, and you will be rewarded handsomely.

e. Assess, reflect, and repeat these actions every time fear grips you, and you will improve over time.

When you learn how to manage fear in the Hallway, you will become more resilient. When I learned how to manage fear, my life changed exponentially. You have the ability to do the same thing!

The Hallway: Hurt or Help

One of the biggest reasons I wrote this book is that I'm always asked how I pushed past the grief and trauma to go on to laugh, smile, and find joy.

I have looked into the faces of women when they ask me that question, and I've read their e-mails and social media private messages. I knew they desperately wanted to find peace and joy for themselves. While I know they wanted a simple and quick answer, life doesn't work that way.

This knowledge of the Hallway didn't appear overnight. In the past, I stayed in Hallways for years at a time, mourning, grieving, punishing myself, and letting my health take a backseat to the pain and sadness I was holding onto. It took time for me to consciously choose to be okay with myself and practice self-care, even in times of grief.

I had to work on getting through the Hallway, just like anyone else. We all have our imbalances, and mine was self-deprivation. Whenever I got upset or received bad news or the unexpected happened, my taste buds would shut down. I can't explain that reaction, but my health declined because I didn't want to eat. Now I realize that not eating was a choice—maybe it was to punish myself—even if stress affected my sense of taste.

We make choices all the time when we're in the Hallway, often unconsciously or out of habit. That is why it's so important to stay aware and really think about what you're doing and why. Then work through the stages of grief, so you are moving forward toward a better life rather than rolling backward into the darkness or getting stuck.

The Hallway can hurt you or help you. You can get lost in it or grow and reach everything you want to be in life. What I want you to remember most is to be patient with yourself. Give yourself a break when you feel like you're not moving quickly enough during your recovery in the Hallway.

When you choose life and are willing to do the work, the choices you make will shape your life and unlock the doors at the end of the Hallway.

When I changed my outlook through gratitude, my life turned around, and it was easier for me to make it through the Hallways in my life. Daily irritations seemed to stop happening so often, or maybe I just had the resilience to brush them off my shoulders. Having a different outlook changes the entire world around you. The universe gave my gracious energy back to me because I was putting positive energy out there. So much good came back to me and fueled my spirit.

Taking the time to approach your emotions with gratitude will change your life. Making decisions with a positive outlook will bring you abundance and energy in return. And that is what you will need to unlock the doors of the Hallway!

Micro Moves to Keep from Getting Stuck

How do you eat an elephant? One bite at a time, one taste at a time, and if you can't handle that—one lick at a time is good enough. The same is true while moving through the Hallway. Take one micro move at a time.

The steps you take in the Hallway will add up to something powerful and important. It's much easier to achieve when you do it in baby micro moves. And when you repeat these actions over time—like working through the Seven Doors—it will help you grow and become more efficient in handling future Hallways. This process is good. It's healthy.

Build a Morning Routine That Focuses on the Positive

Here's the routine I use to bring me strength. Getting into this routine every day will also help keep you from flying off the handle when things don't go your way, shying away from physically and emotionally challenging situations, or escaping into behaviors that don't serve you.

The routine starts when you get up.

◆ Stretch and breathe! Inhale big deep breaths! Be aware of your surroundings. Get into your body. Feel, smell and really see everything. Appreciate the fact that you are able to do that simple task.

◆ Consciously feel and flex every muscle in your body, and smile!

◆ Ask yourself, "What can I do today to make today a great day?"

◆ Write down or record a list of answers to this question.

◆ Set your intentions for your day and decide to make the day a good one.

◆ Meditate or go on a walking meditation

Taking any of these small steps will free up space in your mind to see new and positive things. With a positive attitude, you can change your very existence! You will see opportunities you couldn't have imagined otherwise instead of headaches you can't get over. Life's challenges look smaller, and your chances of succeeding look larger!

Those few moments of gratitude will give you more energy, release stress, and show you the path forward. You begin to feel like life is worth it, and you can achieve your goals, whether it's to get a new job, lose weight, or just get through the day.

By taking just a few moments to see the good around you, even in the darkest of Hallways, you will yearn to be better, and for the first time, genuinely believe you can be. You are more likely to spend the entire day with a smile on your face. When you love your days, you create the possibility to love other things and people again. When I'm asked what I have done to open my heart and see the good after an unpleasant situation, I tell them my life changed once I focused on the positives.

When you improve your outlook, you improve your health. When you improve your health, you can change your life and body forever!

Name Your Feelings

A lot of the emotions you will feel in the Hallway can be identified as one of the Seven Doors to Healing:

1. Disbelief
2. Disown/Disavow
3. Guilt/Regret
4. Outrage/Negotiation
5. Sadness/Despair
6. Adapt/Accept
7. Embrace and prepare to return to the Hallway

When you can pinpoint where you are in this process, you are on your way to processing your emotions. Don't be ashamed! It's normal to be in denial when you experience grief! It's normal to feel anger, question why this happened to you, or feel sad and depressed. It's normal to be in the Hallway, but you must work through these stages to feel better.

Working through your feelings starts with naming your emotions. When you do this, they won't have such a painful sting. You have power over them, and you can process them on *your* time.

Take a moment right now—let's take this micro step together. How are you feeling right now? Yell it out, write it down, text it to a friend or yourself. How are you feeling? Depressed? Excited? Nervous? Angry? *There is no wrong answer.* You can look through a list of emotions to help you name what's going on right now.

After you name your feelings, you might want to sit with yourself and take it all in. Breathe. Then see what comes up for you next. What other emotions can you identify? When I'm sad, I like to share positive affirmations with myself or sit in prayer. When I get anxious, I like to meditate. When I'm feeling pretty good, I keep pushing through. Each feeling you experience is an opportunity to progress and unlock the many doors in the Hallway.

Set Goals and Find Something to Look Forward To

You have one job while you're in the hallway: confront and process your emotions. This is a powerful job to take on, but you don't have to look at it as a daunting journey. The hallway makes it possible for you to go from one place to the other—that's all the hallway is!

Think about the hallways in your house. You don't hang out in the hallways of your home, but you know you have to use them in order to get to the bathroom, the bedroom, or the front door. How are you able to go from room to room without spending too much time in the hallway? It's likely because you know where you're going! You have a reason to walk into the bathroom, bedroom, or home office. This is how you get yourself out of the Hallways of your life: You have a reason to keep walking. And if you don't have that reason right now, take time now to find it! Find something that drives you wild with curiosity, makes you smile or laugh, or something you've been meaning to explore. What can you look forward to?

Believing in a higher power can also help you in your darkest times. Faith or spirituality keeps us going because it's something greater than ourselves. Reach out to people for help: a therapist, a coach like myself, a librarian, or a counselor in your community. We can give you materials, help you look at the Hallway in a whole new way, and shine a light on possibilities to help you advance and grow.

Many websites and community programs offer free resources and information that can help you. Public libraries are full of self-help, nutrition, mental health, and other information that can show you the way. There are also plenty of in-person and online support groups that can become a point of connection and a way to find encouragement and resources.

CHAPTER 6

Surviving the Hallway

---

*"You must tell yourself, 'No matter how hard it is,
or how hard it gets, I'm going to make it.'"*

—Les Brown

Surviving the Hallway is a bitch, and it takes resilience to get through it. But you *can* do it!

Can you imagine what it would be like if you didn't evolve or change? You'd still be wearing diapers. You'd still be sucking your thumb and having temper tantrums. Learning to crawl and then to walk and run takes a lot of falling down and getting up, as every parent knows. But despite that frustration, children press on, and those early triumphs make all the other progress possible which again proves how resiliency is born in you.

What if you didn't evolve or grow? You'd be stuck and couldn't experience the beautiful things you do today.

This process of confronting your emotions is good. It's healthy. It's inevitable. And oh, by the way, it keeps you relevant! To stay relevant, you have to undergo some changes and navigate some hallways. The record player isn't relevant anymore; eight-tracks aren't relevant anymore. Blu-rays, CDs, cassettes—we're in the digital age now. If you're still holding onto eight-tracks, you're going to have a much harder time playing your music where you want to. If you're still holding onto old emotions, you're going to have a much harder time staying healthy, living freely, and creating healthy relationships.

One of the biggest lessons is to learn to adapt and adjust your expectations without feeling like a failure. That is crucial. Don't set rigid deadlines for yourself to complete one phase or another. Life doesn't work that way. If you move through a stage and then cycle back to it, that's part of healing. The second time you return to a stage you aren't the same as you were the first time. You bring what you've already learned with you, so you will deal with that stage differently and learn something new. Don't chastise yourself for it. Sometimes just getting to "almost there" is a *big* thing. The Hallway may feel like a roller coaster ride, but it gradually levels out as you get closer to the end.

The Game Changer

The Hallway asks a lot of you. It asks you to be strong, process intense emotions, and push past some of your greatest fears. But you don't have to come out of the Hallway feeling like damaged goods. You can step out into the light with lessons that will strengthen you for the rest of your life.

There are some basic survival skills that you need to know and should pack away as a part of your first aid kit. These skills will keep you strong, help you survive the Hallway and help you master the art of resiliency.

Let's Review:

- **Be Self-Aware**—it gets the ball rolling and starts you off in the right direction. Without it you remain lost.

- **Use Gratitude**—it helps to enrich your spirit.

- **Find Courage**—Push beyond your comfort zone and do whatever it takes to ensure your livelihood and achieve your wildest dreams! Courage is fearing what's ahead but charging on anyway. Like the day I ran from my abuser, I was scared to death. But I did it. That's courage. My babies screamed uncontrollably, tears rolled down my face, and my heart nearly pounded out of my chest, but I pushed through it and did it anyway! Was it the end of my Hallway? No, it was just the beginning. But it was still an act of courage, and it brought me one step closer to mastering the art of resilience. Remember, resilience is the art of getting back up every time you get knocked down.

- **Redefine Fear**—Challenge the Fear. Understand that it's okay and normal to be afraid. Everyone fears something in life, but don't let it paralyze you. Redefine fear this way: Have it be your "go" button instead of your "stop, run, or hide" button. When you feel fear, (1) first slap the devil off your shoulder who is telling you that you are going to die or you can't do it—because you *can*, (2) repeat to yourself out loud fifty times every single day "I can do this" until you do it, and (3) when faced with fear, push on anyway. If you're told no, find another way to push through it.

I remember giving my client, Carol, a task to do that would really improve her life and as her eyes grew large with fear, she said, "Wendy . . . what if I don't make it? I responded, "What if you *do* make it?"

Don't bet against yourself. Let's push through the fear together and give yourself a chance to grow and win. And I say to you too—give yourself a chance!

- ◆ **Be Creative**—When we're exposed to new things through change and opportunity, we open up and allow ourselves to grow. Creativity will reduce stress, shift you into another gear, and blow up any obstacles in your way.

  Change becomes easier to handle when you're creative. For example—start a new craft project or go back to something you used to enjoy and haven't done for a while. Cook, sing, play music, do art projects, garden—whatever you enjoy. Notice how you feel.

- ◆ **Identify an Outlet**—Identifying an outlet can be a real lifesaver. It should be a safe place where you can emotionally talk through the changes in your life with a trusted mentor, therapist, support group, or community. Using your creativity can reveal more outlets to you and help you process your emotions through art, music, dance, or other creative pursuits.

- ◆ **Lead with Self-Care**—Caring for the body, getting proper rest, eating well, spending time in the sunlight, taking warm baths, going on nature walks, and reading a good book are just a few activities that become even more important during stressful times. They help you to form a healthy foundation from which you can call forth grit, strength, and resiliency.

I know traveling through the Hallway can be challenging but you have to trust yourself. Trusting ourselves can be very difficult when we know we've failed ourselves too many times to count. But you have to give yourself a chance to do better, over and over again. That's what resilience is. When you fall down seven times, get up eight times, and you will eventually get what you want.

When I first started on my journey toward healing and my mentor gave me something to work on so I could improve, I listened and took the ball and ran with it. I didn't sit around or start slowly. I threw myself into the next step wholeheartedly because I was tired of feeling bad about myself. **Your desire to change must be greater than your desire to stay the same.** You have to have a strong determination to move on, and that will light your fire.

Sometimes people know what to do but they don't do it. That's usually because they're afraid of failing. Or maybe they're afraid of succeeding, that if they do get what they want, they will somehow mess it up. Doing the internal work we've been talking about in his book will help you break free of those fears so you can create the life you want.

Keeping your promise to yourself to build a better life is part of the resilience that will help you achieve that goal.

Preparing for the Next Hallway

Hallways are a constant part of life. We are always coming from somewhere and going to somewhere else, and in between are Hallways and transitions, big and small. Preparing for the next one is smart—in fact, it's part of resilience.

There is so much strength to be found in the Hallway. And once you survive this one, you'll be stronger and better prepared to face the next one. Whether or not you identified past struggles and transitions as a Hallway moment, that's what they were. What you learned from them—positively or negatively—provides insight for your current struggle.

Preparation is key to succeed in anything. Whether you are preparing for a party, a performance, a job interview, or a disaster like a hurricane or earthquake, the better you prepare the more likely you are to achieve the outcome you want. Preparing for the next Hallway is no different.

Here's how you can do that. Start with the following three steps.

Step I. Accept That You Will Be Uncomfortable

Whether your Hallway is big or small, accept that you will be uncomfortable in it and understand that discomfort is a sign of progress. Most people run away from discomfort, which hinders their ability to grow. If you've ever tried a new routine at the gym or started a new sport (or anything new), you know there's a lot of discomfort at first as your muscles get used to new challenges. Working through that phase is the only way to get what you want; it feels so good when you achieve your goal and the discomfort changes to capability and confidence.

When you accept that you will be uncomfortable, your psyche prepares you for the ride and you're less likely to freak out. It's like warming up before exercise. You warm up to prepare your mind and body for the journey.

I remember a lady who would always jump right into her workout without warming up, even though I warned her not to do that. She would say, "I don't have time." Eventually she learned an important lesson because she ripped her Achilles tendon. After she recovered from that injury, she *made* time to warm up.

Make time for yourself or you will be forced to take time to visit the doctor. Get comfortable being uncomfortable. Stop fighting the discomfort and ask what it is trying to teach you. When you fight the discomfort, you increase your stress levels and that takes a toll mentally and physically. Once you accept that new situations and transitions—including growing and healing—start out feeling uncomfortable, you can accept the lessons the experience is teaching you, which builds resilience.

Stop thrashing, take a deep breath, let go, and ask yourself what you need to learn in this moment.

Give yourself permission to be uncomfortable. It's okay not to know what's going to happen next. Zone out and let yourself just be, without feeling shame or guilt. Quiet moments when we let our minds rest are often when we get our best ideas. Once you learn to accept feeling uncomfortable and realize that's it is the necessary first step to making a breakthrough, you will embrace it. In doing so, you will build resilience, reduce your fear, find more joy, and build more success in your life.

Step II. Get Clear on What You Have Control Over

What you *do* have control over is *you*! You control your attitude, how open-minded you are, and whether you stay or leave. You control your decisions, your choice of what you want to do next, and how you want to make that happen, given the changes going on in your life.

What you can't control are other people's actions. Most people avoid accepting this truth because they want to keep doing what they've always done (that didn't work)—trying to force other people or their environment into being what they want. It's a way to avoid taking responsibility for taking the steps within your power.

You can't force other people to change. But isn't that what we do all the time? We try to change people and try to control what they want and tell them how they should make their decisions. But the reality is—you can't. I have been guilty of that in the past, and that frustration is so painful and completely futile.

When you are not clear on what you can control, your health suffers because of the unnecessary stress. Mine certainly did. Trying to control something that you can't will get you stuck in the Hallway. It leads to a vicious cycle of pain and frustration.

Step III. Decide How You Want to Grow

See the Hallway as an opportunity and a gift because it is a blessing in disguise. And ultimately, view the Hallway of change as a life lesson. The Hallway is where you come to find meaning and purpose in what you are experiencing, which builds your resilience by giving you something to work toward. Look for what you need to learn or look at differently, so you can reframe your disappointment into an opportunity.

For example, instead of saying, "My business is changing," or "My health is failing, and I don't like it," say, "How am I going to change given that change is at my doorstep?"

It might be, "I'm leaving because I don't want to do this, but I'm going to grow somewhere else." Or you might say, "This is an opportunity of a lifetime to try something different."

In the Hallway, you can also learn to recognize opportunities that might have been invisible to you because of prior programming or voices in your head. People may have told you negative things about yourself—that you're not smart enough, strong enough, or talented enough. If you believed those people, those voices take up permanent residence in your head, and they keep repeating those negative messages long after the people who started the problem are gone.

Because you buy into those negative beliefs, your brain refuses to see opportunities that are right in front of you. You don't think you can do something, so your brain "protects" you by not even letting you try. When you identify and root out those old negative messages and replace them with confidence and resilience, you will see all kinds of new possibilities within your reach!

You get to choose, and you have to decide. That may sound scary, but it sets you free. I choose and decide my own fate every time I go through the Hallway. I'm so glad I trusted myself—my gut, my intuition—and plunged forward despite fear. Making that choice has paid off every time, and I am happier today as a result. Those choices and decisions helped me find my self-worth and saved my life. The resilience I gained gave me the strength to do what I didn't think I was capable of doing. The Hallway is responsible for the woman I am today.

Whenever you feel uncomfortable, search for the gifts and look for the lessons. Knowing where you *do* have control will make your stress plummet and your health soar! You'll be able to handle the Hallway and so much more. You'll start making better decisions because your mind will be sharper, clearer, and more focused. You'll feel less tired, disorganized, and stressed out. And most of all, you'll feel better about you!

Be open to establishing new habits frequently. Doing so means growth and helps you get comfortable with the uncomfortable. Change is a part of life. Now that you know how to deal with being uncomfortable and navigate the Hallway, it's time to embrace change because you know it's an opportunity to grow and become stronger.

We should never stop learning, growing, and moving forward, even when doing so pushes us out of our comfort zone. The thing you have to continually monitor is movement. Are you moving forward or are you in the same place after five or ten years? Do a self-check periodically.

I am so much better than I used to be because of the skills I have mastered in the Hallway. I was put to the test recently, and I had to dig into my skill box. I needed to remind myself that gratitude is the key to finding light in the darkness to lift my spirits and help me make it through.

Using Gratitude to Survive

After thirty-three years with the love of my life, I was thrown into the Hallway with my second divorce, and it seemed a hundred miles long. When I tell you it rained and poured, it's the truth because a chain of events caved in on me during the same time.

My fur baby, Princess, died. She was a two-pound Yorkshire terrier that I called my therapy dog. My roof fell in on me. I discovered major mold issues in my bathrooms. Pigeons and another animal got caught in my attic and wreaked havoc. I also got the news that two cousins died, George Floyd, Black Lives Matter, and political unrest. Need I say more?

If that wasn't enough, one day when I came home, I thought I was in one of those old scary movies by Alfred Hitchcock or the Twilight Zone because there were things crawling out of one of the bathroom toilets—no, it wasn't a snake—they were king-sized water bugs, armies of them. I think those uninvited guests thought there was a party going on.

I can uneasily chuckle about it now (because I still feel traumatized by them) but I can't even describe the horror!

That was the last straw! Talk about trauma after trauma. I was spent! I got pretty sick. Panic attacks, headaches, body aches, and the like because of the burden of all those things happening at the same time. Don't know how I'm still standing.

I was lonely but had to find a new normal. Each time I got up in the morning, everything felt weird and uncomfortable. I was cold and angry, and I wondered if I could go on. I never imagined this for myself. It was the first time I had truly been alone in my life. I discovered that I didn't know how to function at a solo pace.

There I was facing the Hallway again. I wallowed in my pain. At first, I doubted that I could make it through, which created stress. Heart palpitations followed, then hair loss and headaches, which led to not eating or drinking enough. That caused dehydration and near-fainting spells, allergy flare-ups, and muscle aches. Depression also made me lose focus. I forgot to turn off the stove and left the door unlocked—simple things I never would have missed in normal times. I felt bad about myself, and that made it hard to get out of bed. It was hard to muster the will to push onward, and I felt like I was fading fast. There I was again, feeling broken and in deep despair!

Then suddenly, I cried out, "Lord, I want to live!" With those words in that very moment, something was lifted off of my chest and body; not only did some of the physical pain go away, but mentally there was a clearing. He answers prayers, I tell you.

In that moment, I realized that I'm never alone. I must remain resilient and strong no matter how low I go, I told myself. I'm on a journey, and these feelings are part of stretching and growing in many beautiful ways.

Finally, one morning I found myself at the end of the Hallway, entering a new chapter of my life and finding a new normal. I found myself eager to get up in the morning and begin my day. I was grateful for everything I went through because I found some diamonds along the way that made me laugh and kept me afloat. Prayer and gratitude were a big part of my survival in that Hallway.

During that whole process, I used self-care to increase my resilience. I created happy moments and rituals, took long baths, preserved historic family memories, and found ways to reinforce and strengthen positivity.

One of my favorite family memories was when our family took cruises together. One of them was a wedding cruise. We went all out. Got top of the line suites, concierge treatment and indulged in a variety of luxurious activities. But some of the best times were simple like the time we had ladies' night out. We went to a party, and I let loose. I was filled with joy and so happy to be surrounded with love and family that I couldn't control myself.

My family knows I can go overboard when I'm happy. So true to self, while I was dancing, I challenged people I didn't even know to a dance off and we got wild and crazy. It led to me jumping down on the dance floor in my diva dress and heels to do push-ups. The waiter I was dancing with followed my lead and to outdo me, took one foot off the floor with his pushups. I did the same. Then to outdo him I put one arm behind my back—to reiterate, all in my diva dress. By the end of the night my blue dress was soaked, turned gray, and I left a nice puddle of water on the floor at the pizza shop we went to afterwards.

What possessed me to do all of that? I don't know. But by the end of the cruise everyone was calling me trouble.

We still talk and laugh about those good times today. And if I'm sad on any given day, this is one of the memories I think about. It makes me smile, I feel the joy all over again, and it helps me survive another day.

Growing and stretching are all part of my journey. The happy memories and rituals I created for myself along the way when I was barely able to walk or crawl through the Hallway are what I call my pacifiers—just like what a baby uses for comfort—because these simple actions comforted me. For example, one of my clients gave me fun little wine glasses that I like to fill with Perrier sparkling mineral water. I bring a glass to the bathtub, set up my bath pillow and my tray, turn on spa music, light my aroma therapy candles, and just relax. I love to put lavender, Epsom salt, and bubbles in my bath to soothe me when I need to rest and recover. One of my newest pacifiers is a weighted blanket. It not only makes me sleep better, but it makes me feel secure and swaddled like a baby. Those things console me, bring me peace, and help me take positive steps forward.

Surviving the Hallway requires that you take care of yourself along the way. Rest. Care for your body. Recognize opportunities to slow down and draw on gratitude. When you're in the Hallway, you can learn to see everything in a new light because you control how you see things. Find opportunities to say, "thank you" and stay in deep gratitude. This will help you move just a bit further even on the toughest days.

Making those choices for yourself is what resilience is all about. I chose to do the work to heal and then followed my purpose, and it has healed my soul and allowed my spirit to shine. That's resilience. With each new Hallway, I continue to gain resilience, and as a result, I am open to love and have become so much stronger.

Micro Moves to Survive the Hallway

The work begins with micro moves that make you feel good and encourage you. All of my micro moves and big moves together will get you through the Hallway, stronger and better than before!

Practice Getting Comfortable with the Uncomfortable

Actively pursue activities that put you outside of your comfort zone. For example, if you are shy or anxious in big crowds, work up to larger events or meetings to gain confidence. Force yourself to talk and interact with others.

Start with exposing yourself to this situation for ten minutes at a time or talking to just one person and then leave. A little temporary discomfort can help you grow and adapt. Even small but repeated decisions to let yourself be uncomfortable can add up. Eventually, you will become a stronger and more confident person.

Get Rid of Negative Chatter

Free yourself by fanny-slapping the devil on your shoulder that keeps telling you that you aren't good enough or you won't survive and repeat affirmations to yourself to flood out the devil.

Celebrate Small Wins

Celebration doesn't have to be a grand party or an international vacation. You can celebrate in many small ways, like buying a lovely outfit for yourself that you've always wanted. Celebration can be booking yourself a nice massage. You can also celebrate by giving yourself a pat on the back! Big or small, celebrations are a form of self-gratitude that help you build your resilience.

Also, you can:

◆ Take a walk to a place that makes you feel safe.

◆ Enjoy a foot bath.

◆ Schedule an appointment with your therapist.

◆ Do a particular workout with all your favorite moves that make you feel strong and energized.

Not every day will be a big leap forward. But the important thing to remember is to take care of your health while in the Hallway so you can be strong and resilient when you reach the other side.

PART THREE

Reclaim

WENDY'S WISDOM:

*Detox from revenge fantasies and use that energy
on positive actions that help you grow.*

CHAPTER 7

Reclaim Your Strong and Sexy

"For what it's worth: it's never too late to be whoever you want to be. I hope you live a life you're proud of, and if you find that you're not, I hope you have the courage to start over again."

—F. Scott Fitzgerald

Sometimes what we perceive as a bad thing is really a blessing in disguise. That's how it was for me when I began my journey to reclaim my strong and sexy.

I started out as a fast-food junkie and thought I was doing well. I'd eat my veggies out of a can, and I'd feed my kids that way too. I made excuses for how I ate and couldn't understand why I felt sick and tired most of the time. I blamed a lot of it on family history. My sister and I often sat around and talked about how we were destined to be overweight like the people in our family from the previous generation.

I tried different ways to lose weight and improve my health, but it didn't work out. My lack of confidence prevented me from getting professional help and that came with stress and guilt that literally changed my personality. I had no motivation, and I was dragging around, dodging past mirrors because I didn't like what I saw. Heck, I didn't even like myself.

The last time I made a promise to myself to take care of myself I got halfway there and decided to give up. But then I got sick and tired of being sick and tired.

That's when I met my earth angel (a fitness professional) who helped me discover and develop a new strength that I didn't know I had. This earth angel showed me what I was missing, rerouted my thinking, and changed my life forever.

I discovered the secrets to how my mind and body communicated through fitness and healthy living. As I embarked on a new journey and began to reinvent my life, my body, mind, and spirit came alive. I rediscovered myself and made changes I never thought were possible. Each step of the way, I created encouraging results, and with each step, I began to recognize my power. My confidence grew; I got stronger and felt sexier than ever! I lost eighty pounds and had more energy than ever! I cleared the clutter in my brain and transformed my body completely.

As a result, I started making better choices. I learned that strength is essential if you want to live a long and good quality of life. It's essential to successfully work your way through the Hallway of change. It builds confidence, dissipates fear, and promotes resilience. Your emotional, mental, and physical health depend on it. I am grateful to have discovered who I was really born to be.

Before   **After**

The greatest gift, however, was when I realized that this awakening in me was so much bigger than I imagined. Because I was rescued by an angel that transformed my life, I also was blessed with the opportunity to be an earth angel for someone else. It hit me like a ton of bricks in a good way. I realized that we are all here to play a part in transforming lives and changing the world.

Becoming Someone's Earth Angel

I was working at an upscale sports club as a personal trainer when I met Vincent. I thrived in this atmosphere and took great pride in changing other people's lives. I just didn't realize how much it meant to them as well until Vincent spoke up and wrote this note to me on a piece of paper.

"Worked out by an angel.

"That's how I describe Wendy Ida to my friends. For the last twenty years, I have fought a battle with arthritis, lower back pain, bad knees, and most recently, I was in a car accident. After the accident, I believed all I could do was manage the pain and atrophy of my muscles. And then I met my angel. Wendy showed me that I could, can, and will get stronger. She rekindled the desire to have fun by working out intelligently and making progress in stages. The workouts are challenging enough that I feel successful every time. Her attitude is wonderful, and she always has a smile and an encouraging word to say. Most importantly, she made me feel like she cared about my progress and that my goal, when I met her, was too low, and that I could do much more. And she was right.

Thank you, Wendy."

—Vincent D.

"People will forget what you said, people will forget what you did, but people will never forget how you made them feel."

—Maya Angelou

Although I've received many testimonials since then, Vincent's note was the first one so it's special! Isn't our first of most experiences in life very special? I keep it as a reminder of how far I've come and the lives I've changed along the way.

As I help others change their lives, the testimonials have continued to come in. It gives me so much joy and reinforces that I am living my purpose. It is why I say to you, "Go for it and never give up." Anything and everything *is* possible!

Unbreaking JJ

JJ was stepping into the Hallway when I first met her. She was a corporate headhunter making six figures, but she hated her job. She wanted out; she wanted a life change. I could tell she was in trouble, and I set out to help her through the dramatic transformation she needed. By the end of the year, she had entered a bodybuilding competition, won trophies, left her job, changed her career, and decided she wanted to follow the same path I was on—including doing speaking events.

One of the great things about JJ that made it all work is that she was very coachable. She showed up, did the work, trusted the process, followed my instruction, and changed habits that didn't serve her well. JJ was so excited about her progress and life changing experience that she wrote this:

> *"Wendy is absolutely one of the most dynamic, insightful, and as you most likely already know, beautiful women I have ever had the privilege of meeting!*
>
> *"As a founder and VP of Talent Acquisition for Imagine IT, Inc., I interact with hundreds of people yearly from around the planet. My position provides me a unique perspective into people types, what motivates them, and even more importantly what they have to contribute to our world. Wendy Ida is someone divinely appointed and perfectly equipped to deliver her many gifts.*
>
> *"So, how did I find Wendy? Near my fortieth birthday, I began feeling less than excited about my life. As one of those A+ personality types, I was drained from imbalances I'd allowed by overexerting myself professionally and personally. I needed a boost and started searching. Somehow,*

109

I stumbled on her book, Take Back Your Life. I read it end-to-end and immediately reached out to schedule our first consult. From call one, I knew I was on to something extraordinary. Still, my intent was to attend a few 1:1s, learn some exercises, and continue on my own. A year and a half later, I've only just moved on from consistent 3x weekly 1:1 sessions. I've kept Wendy on speed dial, and I'm now strutting across stages with the fittest of the fit in bedazzled bikinis winning first place trophies at muscle contests. Not bad for a new hobby! In all, I've enjoyed exponential growth in all areas of wellness; my confidence is through the roof, and I've learned to cultivate an inexhaustible source of power. You can too if you trust Wendy with you!

"Since completing my first round of training with Wendy, I've spent more than a bit of time trying to nail down exactly what she did to bring me away from that funk I was heading for. Was it something specific she said? An exercise she taught that somehow unblocked a clogged channel inside? Was it the motivation she imparted when I realized this sixty-plus-year-old beauty could outdo me in any squat, burpee, press, lift, or other routine she created for me? Yes, yes, yes, and then some.

"During our training, I was also being mentored emotionally and challenged to mature as a woman, mother, and wife. What?! When did she sneak that in? I recall countless instances where Wendy helped me identify and conquer perceived challenges to my physical and muscle development; challenges that truthfully had little or nothing to do with my physicality. Her approach to fitness and coaching is comprehensive. Though you may connect with a specific goal in mind, Wendy can tailor your program to

include everything necessary for continued success. You just need to trust her, be honest, and follow her instructions impeccably. Trust her wealth of experiences as a wellness consultant, nutritionist, fitness champion, Guinness Book World record holder, motivational speaker, actress, world traveler, and model (to name a few). These achievements provide her sensibilities and insight few in her field can offer. Wendy will deliver big time!

"She'll teach you to care for your body, beginning with the way you think. She will also provide you a sustainable foundation of knowledge and confidence to support and encourage continued growth when you're ready to move on. Folks, this woman is truly a goddess among mortals. I am so thankful to have invited her into my life. I hope you do too!"—JJ

After working with so many people, here's what I know and what I have said to my clients. Everyone has a different lifestyle and is motivated by different things, but regardless of what your age is, where you come from, or what you've been through, it's possible to make your life better as long as you are willing to do the work. And if you are willing, I will help you get there.

Unbreaking Bonnie

Bonnie was a fifty-one-year-old morbidly obese six- to seven-hundred-pound woman who had lived in her bed between five to six years. She never left it for anything. She ate, slept, and did her business there. Regardless of how many years she spent in bed, it's important to note that her life took a turn for the worse due to a chain of disturb-

ing life events that thrust her in the Hallway and kept her stuck there for years. Bonnie's spiral downhill began in her forties and her family thought she would die there, but she was inspired to move out of the Hallway and out of her bed to start living again because of the birth of her grandson. That's when I got the call.

A producer at BBC Worldwide TV said, "We need help." I was honored to be there for them. I worked with Bonnie for months. We worked on emotional balance, mental strengthening, and physical conditioning. We made great progress in stages and Bonnie was strong enough to sit up and do more. Some of the swelling in her legs had decreased, and she was feeling more hopeful. But at a certain point, it became too dangerous to continue because Bonnie's bed was not stable enough and to continue might have jeopardized her life.

With Bonnie's permission, I had firefighters and EMTs build a new bed for her. Bonnie went to a whole new level after that. We did more, and she got better. Finally, with her new energy and spirit, she gave the okay to remove her from the bed and ultimately cut her out of that house for good. It was emotional. It was amazing, and I will never forget her face and her tears of joy. Not only was she glad to be out of bed but to see her gloat and feel the joy of sunlight on her face was priceless.

The Iyanla Vanzant show showcased Bonnie's story and some of my work with her.

Vincent, JJ, and Bonnie are just a few people who have been able to rebuild their lives and reclaim their strong and sexy. I am proud to be a part of their success. Clients and fans from all over the world can relate to their stories. Every day, I hear from people who are making changes to their diet, exercise routine, and lifestyle, and they too are seeing results! These people come from all backgrounds and all ages, and they seem to have one mindset in common: after they see what is possible, they are inspired to believe that they can achieve the same success.

Strength is Resilience

Strength is essential! Strength is sexy! Strength is meaningful to everything about you! It provides a good quality of life, helps you manage Hallways of change, gives you confidence to push through your fears, and more. Without it, not only will your body atrophy but your entire life will trickle downhill too.

It doesn't matter what age you are; improving your strength has many benefits that will enrich the quality of your life. But keep in mind that we are not just talking about physical strength or what you do in the gym. It goes deeper. Even more than strengthening your mind and spirit. As Mahatma Gandhi would say,

"Strength does not come from physical capacity. It comes from an indomitable will."

So how do we build strength? There are several ways. There are games, rituals, and exercises that I recommend you do daily to ensure healthy growth. You can use my micro workout moves, nutritional guidance, and my other mental, spiritual and lifestyle rituals to help you begin your process. Whether you are just building strength or muscle, interested in weight loss, or just maintaining good health, it is an excellent place to start.

Fun fact—while strong is the new sexy, research shows that increasing your strength not only increases your sexual desire, but it also increases your ability to enjoy and perform sex safely too.

The following chapters will help you build new habits and structure to ensure you'll grow stronger and more resilient. If you have one minute, five minutes, or ten minutes—that's all it takes to get started! Just start where you are, begin with what you have, and do the little you can do. I encourage you to proceed slowly to ensure success.

After you've reached some milestones, pushed through adversities, and regained healthier and more functional habits, I promise you'll see results.

Age Is Not a Factor

I remember thinking, "I'm over the hill. It's too late to start life over." That song played in my head for about ten years. I wasted a lot of time and energy doing nothing because I didn't think I had any control over my destiny and my happiness. "Why should I take care of myself?" That was my big question.

I had bought into the old idea of what society thought about aging. I thought age was a negative thing. I noticed as people got older, they became invisible, neglected, and forgotten. Jobs all around me in the media and in the corporate world reinforced that sentiment because older people were being replaced by their younger counterparts.

As a result of these observations, I felt ashamed and didn't want to get older. I had what I call the "Peter Pan" syndrome. If you've ever seen the classic movie *Peter Pan,* you know what I'm talking about. It's about a boy who never wants to grow up. So, he goes to a place called "Never Never Land" where you never have to grow up.

But you know what? Just because we were conditioned to be ashamed of aging doesn't mean things have to stay that way. News flash: The outdated thinking that you are useless and sexless as you get older is a myth!

For me it was a gradual process, but I finally stopped caving into those old ways of thinking and instead created my own vision with new goals and no limits. Despite age and how old I felt (I was in my mid-forties at the time) I took a chance and began strengthening my body, mind, and soul, and it turned my whole life around. That's when I learned that age is just a number, and regardless of age, you can improve your health, strength, and happiness.

What keeps this all in perspective for me is that my mother wasn't here for long. She died at forty-two; my sister passed at forty-nine. I know for sure that they would love to be here celebrating another birthday. So, I am careful not to take my age for granted. I am grateful to be able to celebrate my age with every passing year. And I realize the importance of working on myself to stay strong mentally and physically every day.

I talk to clients, friends, and fans about this all the time. They have all hidden their age or thought of it negatively at some point, but I am proud to say that with each passing year, I find more people taking back their power, changing their mindsets, and realizing that they are capable of much more. And now they are improving their lives regardless of age.

Celebrate yourself and let there be no shame in your game. Change that attitude into gratitude and enjoy what's possible.

When you live everyday like there's no tomorrow with purpose and passion, it extends your life even more. It's never too late!

Using Wisdom to Gain Strength

Gaining strength can help you age gracefully and aging gracefully is a sign of resilience if you are aging wisely. The reality is not everybody who gets older gets wiser. Some people get bitter and get stuck in the past, which can lead to depression. When you get stuck, you become inflexible and rigid and can easily break down. That is contrary to what resilience and longevity represents.

Resilience requires flexibility. It requires that you change with the times and adapt to new situations to push through the obstacles. It requires good health and belief in one's ability to handle what life has to offer if you want to keep gaining ground. If you do the work that I recommend in this book, it will keep you moving in the right direction no matter what age you are.

In early childhood, we are judged and made to feel less valuable as we age. Technically, you are more valuable because you have wisdom. Remember—you can only stake claim to your wisdom if you remain flexible and adaptable instead of rigid and stuck. Wisdom is your badge of honor. You've earned it through your experiences in life. You've had ups and downs, heartbreak and joys, aches and pains, and you've learned, grown, and stretched yourself in enormous ways to survive and make your life better. Through the years, you have pushed through fears and complex situations, you have witnessed miracles of life, brought new life to earth, and so much more. Those are signs of resilience and from that wisdom should grow. Those are signs you have pushed through barriers to get to this point in your life. Give yourself praise and credit for surviving to this point. Now we want to make sure you stay healthy.

Even though we are born resilient, we take it for granted when we are young. That's because we don't have to work for it. Nature is on our side. From the time we are born to the age of twenty-five to thirty, we are building muscle and strength without doing a thing. After that time, physical muscle and other things begin to decline, and there is an awakening within us as the body changes. After thirty, nature hands you the baton. Nature is saying, I carried you this far; now it's your turn to take over. Now you have to do some work to maintain your strength and muscle gains. You have to rethink, redefine, and reinvent your approach to everything. How you feel about yourself, what you think, and how you take care of your health are big factors in staying healthy and resilient as you age. This is where the wisdom must come in and be used to build strength.

It's important to get clear on the difference between knowledge and wisdom. Knowledge is simply knowing. Anyone can become knowledgeable about anything by reading, researching, and Googling any subject, but wisdom involves much more. Wisdom gives us a healthy dose of perspective and the ability to make sound judgments by dealing with things in the best possible way to achieve the best results. Wisdom considers all the possibilities that may arise to change the order of priorities and thus change the behavior.

Although nature is not doing the heavy lifting anymore and it becomes apparent that you must do more instead, it may feel like a disadvantage because you're not in the habit of working for some of your desired body goals. But it's not a disadvantage. See it as grace. You've been given a break, and now you just have to learn a new habit, that's all.

The upside? You've got wisdom under your belt and it must now take the lead. With each passing year, it's extremely important to stay connected to the inner wisdom that speaks to you constantly. Building your strength through wisdom will give you the edge.

Knowing is just knowing; wisdom is getting it done!

Negativity and Naysayer Parties

Sometimes we harbor our own negative baggage, but we can change that by cleaning up our internal dialogue. Do a self-evaluation to assess where you are in your life and what thoughts consume most of your day. That way you can make a conscious but informed intelligent shift that fits your lifestyle.

Get rid of the outdated thinking that says because you are older you are less valuable. That's a myth! When you buy into that negativity, it can shorten your life. Depression, loneliness, regret, and the ability to express yourself will take control and make you miserable.

How you see yourself and what you think will affect what you attract into your life. If your outlook is in the dumps, your attitude may stink too. Things like self-doubt or wishing to be like others are red lights. Make a conscious effort to recognize and reroute your mind to think positive things about yourself, and great rewards will come your way.

Look in the mirror. What do you see when nobody's looking? Point out only the things you love about yourself when you look in the mirror and marinate on it for a while. Do it every day. It will build your self-worth. Unless you can see your self-worth, you will attract and put up with *anything*, and you'll always find yourself in situations that reflect low self-belief.

Get rid of external negativity. Start with how you see the world and the people in it. Some people see the world as a beautiful place, filled with good people and opportunities. Others see the world as an unwelcoming, dangerous place where only bad things happen. Take a moment and think about that right now. How have you shown up in your life thus far? Has it been negative or positive? If you are carrying around negative energy, it doesn't matter what happens—you will find something negative and wrong with everything you encounter. If you carry around positive energy, it will enrich your life. The way you see the world will attract situations and circumstances that reflect that vision.

Take a look at the company you keep. Is it negative or positive? When you are trying to make positive changes or do good in the world, naysayers will often be at your doorstep trying to hitch a ride. My mother used to say, "If you lie down with dogs, you'll get up with fleas." Whether it's friends, coworkers, or family, be tough and stand up for yourself. Don't follow the pack. Slowly fade them out of your life. I made a lot of progress when I relieved myself of negative dead weight. But don't just take it from me. A fan from my YouTube channel sent me this message after watching one of my videos.

"Yeah, I needed to see this. I got fit at fifty-eight years old. It took about six months. My blood pressure went from 145/90 to 117/82. I dropped about twenty pounds, and it truly gives you the energy that people would have you believe disappears with age. What a lie! You've got to fight your way through it. You are one of my inspirations. I know Wendy had to have naysayers, and I hope she writes another book about that side of it. You go, Wendy!"—dbm Mathews

Thanks for the shout out dbm Mathews! I'm so glad you are better and didn't let age become a barrier or excuse to live your best life.

Turn those negative thoughts inside out to create a more positive atmosphere. Change how you talk to yourself. Focus on gratitude to help you enjoy beautiful present-day moments. Live with purpose. Keep a good sense of humor and maintain good health. Create long-term relationships, make friends, and engage in social circles. These things will reinforce positive living and encourage resilience.

When you change your thoughts and how you see the world, you feel a sense of peace, and you care less about people judging you.

Micro Moves to Reclaim Your Strong and Sexy

I began my journey thinking, "Go big or go home." I failed every time! It was so frustrating! The problem was that I was listening to commercials, infomercials, fad diets, and quick fixes—they all jacked my body up (and my mind) in different ways. I learned that bigger is not always better real fast. I also learned that the "no pain, no gain" rule is a myth too. Ultimately, I developed a set of micro moves that helped me step into my healthy body and lose the weight!

Be aware that not everyone is on board with this—making small moves. There are still people who may be well-intended but will not value your micro progress. Don't let their negative feedback get you down. I assure you that if you hang in there with me, you will succeed just like some of my past clients. Remember, we are going for longevity and resilience. Just like we've had micro resilience and micro gratitude, micro progress along with micro moves is valuable and valid too. Get started by taking these micro steps.

Compliment the Mirror

Look in the mirror and compliment yourself. At first, you may not feel comfortable complimenting yourself and may not even believe the things you're saying. It's normal to feel that way. Just know that over time you will believe. And as a result, you will improve your confidence and feel better in no time.

Here are some of my favorites to sing, shout, and say each morning, but feel free to make up your own. Say them out loud and proud, write them down, and chant them daily.

- I am worthy.
- I believe in myself and I trust my own wisdom.
- I was born with a unique gift that I'm proud of.
- I have the ability to achieve anything I desire!
- I am beautiful inside and out.
- I love me!
- I have a fit, powerful, healthy body and mind.

Reinforce Your Internal Strength through Outlook

Turn something negative into a positive with these steps:

- Think about an unpleasant story you have seen, heard, or experienced.
- Now replay the story a second time but talk about what you learned from it the second time you tell it.

- ◆ Repeat that exercise by replaying at least two more unpleasant stories in your head, so you start to get the idea.

- ◆ Now apply that mentality to some things happening in your present state of mind.

Remember, how you respond to a situation is more important than what occurred. When things come up whether it is something you don't like about yourself or what someone has done or said to you, always keep in mind that there are two ways to react or look at things—a negative and positive way.

Find Your Inner Child

Aging gracefully and feeling youthful, strong, and resilient can be a lot of fun if you keep the magic of childhood within you.

There's strength in a fun-loving spirit. There's strength in taking risks. Act like a two-year-old and fearlessly risk doing something new—something you've never done before—and the universe will join you to make things happen. It will manifest into opportunities you could never have imagined. For example, try horseback riding, cage flying, skydiving, water rafting, ice skating, etc. It doesn't have to be a sport either. It could also be walking into a room full of people and introducing yourself. For some people, that is very risky. Be safe but risk doing something challenging.

Be Grateful for Your Age

We know the importance of gratitude. List what you are grateful for in your life right now. Start with being grateful that you've achieved your age because it carries its own illustrious label and may signify that you are resilient with each passing year. Include on your gratitude list all the things you can do and then go out and do them. Also, list how you will celebrate and appreciate your next birthday.

Play Games

Get out your crossword puzzles, board games, or card games! It's so much fun to set up a game night. Solving puzzles will keep you mentally sharp and wanting for more of a robust lifestyle. Set up a weekly event and have something silly to look forward to with friends.

CHAPTER 8

Reclaim Your Power

"If we are creating ourselves all the time, then it is never too late to begin creating the bodies we want instead of the ones we mistakenly assume we are stuck with."

—Deepak Chopra

When I started to work out, I wasn't expecting a grand transformation. I just wanted to lose weight, feel better, and maybe look better. I wasn't expecting to quit my job as an accountant and become a fitness guru. I didn't expect to build my own international coaching business, become a speaker, host TV shows, write books, hold two Guinness World Records, or become an eight-time bodybuilding champion.

But with each step in my journey, I felt the power within me. My view and perspective changed at every level. I rose to the top of several areas in my life and morphed into many new and exciting things. At one point, I remember thinking, "What's next for me? I have my degree, I got a better job, I am healthy and happy, but where can I take this next?" Bingo! I wanted to build more muscle and strength, and I wanted to feel sexy again. All of this happened because I started living a healthier lifestyle, but it didn't happen overnight. I took one micro step at a time.

Not everyone wants to be a bodybuilder. Not everyone has to be a bodybuilder. You must choose whatever turns you on. But one thing is for sure—everything should start with a strong and healthy mind and body. That is, of course, if you want to make your dream come true. I started to work on my physical body first; gradually, my mindset showed signs of improvement too. So many people don't understand the importance of staying active until they are older, can't move, or become ill. My aunt Louise was in her eighties when she first realized that working out was her lifeline. During her recovery from an illness, it not only made her feel better but working out and eating right also improved her energy and quality of life. It extended her life. Watching her transformation reinforced my belief that when you build strength, you're building energy, overall health, and of course, resilience.

So, where do you start? To increase your energy and change your lifestyle and longevity, introduce this three-pronged approach to resilience into your daily lifestyle:

- ◆ Strength Eating
- ◆ Strength Conditioning
- ◆ Strength Thinking

Strength Eating

Food is the precursor to strength conditioning. It's important to have good fuel in your body before doing anything. When you eat the right foods, your organs function better, you have a more productive workout, and it helps you achieve more desirable results.

Three Essentials to Maintain Balance and Increase Longevity

Balance is essential when eating meals. It will ensure that you digest and process foods efficiently and help to produce optimal strength and muscle gains. Balance will keep you full, satiated, and energized. Keep yourself balanced with these three essentials: protein, carbohydrates, and good fats.

Protein

Your body requires the proper amount of protein to rebuild and maintain muscle tissue. Many older women and vegans don't get enough protein. Over time, a lack of protein can cause you to lose muscle mass. It can also cut into your strength gains. A lack of protein will slow your metabolism and prevent your body from getting the proper nutritional balance it needs to ensure optimal health. Over time, low protein can lead to anemia (which means your cells aren't getting enough oxygen) and fatigue.

You can improve your health and may even enhance weight loss if you add plant-based meals that include:

◆ Fruits

◆ Vegetables

◆ Nuts

◆ Seeds

◆ Oils

◆ Whole grains

◆ Legumes

◆ Beans

Plant-based foods and proteins provide many other health benefits too such as lowering blood pressure, cholesterol, and blood sugar levels. It reduces the risk of other diseases and reduces inflammation. The best part is that you will sleep better and feel more vibrant!

Whether you add a few plant-based meals throughout the week or go completely plant based, you will see benefits.

Carbohydrates

Carbohydrates (carbs) are our main energy source. They fuel the body and brain, protect our muscles, and feed the bacteria in the gut. The body converts carbohydrates to glycogen, which is stored in your muscles to power your workout.

It's important to note, however, for sustained energy and strength throughout the day, you must eat complex carbs.

Complex (good) carbohydrates are the preferred fuel for most cells in the body. These include:

- Nonstarchy veggies (spinach, green beans, Brussel sprouts, celery, tomatoes, etc.)
- Unrefined whole grains
- Whole wheat
- Brown rice
- Barley
- Quinoa
- Oatmeal

Refined (bad) carbohydrates, in excess, cause weight gain and energy lows. These include:

- Sugar-sweetened beverages

- White bread
- Pastries
- Other items made with white flour

Good Fats

Eat foods with "good" unsaturated fats. Evidence shows that unsaturated fat continues to be the healthiest type of fat. "Good" unsaturated fats—monounsaturated and polyunsaturated fats—lower your risk of disease. Food high in good fats include:

- Vegetable oils (olive, canola, sunflower, soy, and corn)
- Nuts
- Seeds
- Fish

Other fats include:

- Tofu (includes protein and amino acids)
- Avocados
- Dark chocolate
- Whole eggs

Bad Fats

There are two types of bad fats that should be eaten sparingly: saturated and trans-fatty acids. Both can raise cholesterol levels, clog arteries, and increase your risk for heart disease.

- Commercially baked pastries, cookies, doughnuts, muffins, cakes, pizza dough
- Packaged snack foods (crackers, microwave popcorn, chips)

- Stick margarine, vegetable shortening.
- Fried foods (French fries, fried chicken, chicken nuggets, breaded fish)

Be careful! Many people eat excess animal protein, fat, and processed foods, which leads to digestive issues, heart disease, diabetes, and other weight- and diet-related health conditions.

Fact: Good fat burns your body fat. Bad fat stores body fat.

The Cease and Replace Method

Whether you want to start eating healthier or simply incorporate plant-based foods into your diet, use my "Cease and Replace" method. That means replace what you might be eating that's not good for you with something better. For example, if you are drinking soda pop, replace it with something like iced tea. Iced tea is better for you and your body, and it doesn't have all the sugar that soda has. Be careful if you're from the south; Southerners tend to put a lot more sugar in their tea. Try using a natural sweetener like honey or guava instead. Make sure to replace one food at a time.

This is a list of some big culprits you should consider replacing:

- Orange juice—has lots of sugar. Drink sparingly. Replace with hot or iced tea.

- Margarine—this is not a real food; it's synthetic and manifests as heart disease. Replace with grass-fed butter, olive oil, or flaxseed oil.

- Soda—contains many other harmful things besides sugar. Warning: Diet soda is just as bad as regular soda. Replace with iced tea or sparkling water.

◆ Breads—are comfort foods that are quick carbs that store in the belly as fat. Replace with Ezekiel bread or cut it out altogether.

◆ Fried foods—cause heart disease and clogged arteries. Replace with baked, steamed, roasted, or sautéed foods.

You can also cease and replace parts of a meal. For example, replace half of your animal protein with half a cup of quinoa, lentils, or beans. Or, instead of two eggs for breakfast, have one egg and a half cup of beans.

Always start with one thing and get used to that change until you feel good about it and it feels like you've adapted a new habit you can live with. When that happens, you move on to the next food you can cease and replace. This approach will allow your palate to adjust to new taste buds.

That is how I have always done it. I have weaned myself onto a healthy and clean way of living every time by changing one bad habit at a time. But it's not just me. My fans all over the world are experiencing similar results. One of my YouTube fans made this comment after seeing one of my videos.

"I'm fifty-two and been fully plant-based, no oil for six-plus years, and I have no gray hair or wrinkles. Women like you have always been an inspiration. My husband is closer to your age and went fully plant-based a few years ago (except for odd brownie or freshly baked bread). But now, if there's a vegan option, he'll take it. He takes no medication and is guessed at ten years younger. His bloodwork and blood pressure are that of a man half his age. You both have far more energy than me, partly due to my Addison's. We don't avoid gluten and stay with mostly 100 percent

whole grain. We don't deny ourselves, but like you, our tastes have changed for good. Thanks, Wendy."—mc

You too can wean yourself into eating better. Just be patient with yourself and you will start feeling healthier, have more energy, and no doubt grow stronger.

Watch out for diets on the market that deprive you of everything all at once. That never works. The body and mind can't handle the constant feeling of deprivation or too many changes at once.

So, I'm not telling you to stop everything all at once. I'm saying take a fresh breath and new perspective to using my "Cease and Replace" method to help you break those barriers that have long held you back.

Don't Go Overboard

By the way, just because you cease eating something you may have loved in the past doesn't mean you can't ever have that again. You can have anything you want; just don't have it every day. You can have a piece of birthday cake—just don't eat the whole cake! If you celebrate a birthday one day, go back to exactly what you should be doing the next day. You don't want to be the only person not celebrating Thanksgiving by eating a salad; that may make you feel like a weirdo and not part of the celebration. You can have a Thanksgiving dinner. Just do it in small proportions!

People become discouraged if they feel like they are cut off from everything. Things we like to eat are associated with very strong emotions. Food is an emotional connection; it's a mental thing. It gives people hope.

Personally, I never feel deprived at all. Even when I'm training for a competition, I have whatever I want once a week. It's funny when people ask me what I eat or are shocked when they see me eating something like a muffin or pizza. I just laugh and say, "Oh yeah, I like to party too." LOL.

I assure you that once you start making these micro changes, you will feel a different energy and strength that you've never known. And that will motivate you to eat more of the good stuff and less of the stuff that sucks the strength out of you.

Don't Get Caught with Your Pants Down

To always give your body what it needs and when it needs it, meal prep is a good solution. Cook your meals for the week and put each meal in an individual container. When it's time to eat, just pop one out, and you're good to go. If you are traveling, put two to four meals in an insulated bag and throw it in the back of your car. You'll save money, time, and your body from eating the wrong thing.

I also carry protein bars, raisins, nuts, and protein drinks wherever I go for a fast substitute. Whether I'm on the set in the media and especially when I'm traveling, I use my cease and replace method. It provides me with the sustained energy I need for the day. My energy has no peaks and valleys, and when I hit the bed, I get a great night's sleep.

If you don't meal prep to some degree, you may get caught with your pants down. What I mean is you may get caught without food when you really need it. When you are tired and hungry while on the road (for example, in a meeting, in traffic, or running errands) and you don't have good food with you ready to eat, you will suffer. You'll feel cranky and tired, and you won't be able to think or see straight. The other alternative is you'll fall victim to eating at the first fast food place you see—you'll eat anything!

It would be like one of those disaster movies where someone is locked in a cabin in a blizzard, and they've run out of firewood. To keep from freezing to death, they burn the furniture. When you get to that "burn the furniture" place, you're at your low point. You will grab the worst things for you—things like fast foods and sugary treats—that will give you a quick hit of energy and then drop you like a hot potato. Think of a handful of M&M's, cookies, red licorice candy, or potato chips. I always see tons of these snacks when I'm working on a TV production.

Remember, this is a step-by-step journey to make it to the end goals and beyond. Ease into doing a little meal prep and keep repeating that pattern regardless of life's obstacles and you'll get better with practice.

Stay focused. Stay positive. Plan it out and take it moment to moment, day by day.

Reminders:

- Decide to eat consciously versus unconscious
- Apply the cease and replace rule
- Apply the "do it in moderation" rule
- For sustained energy throughout the day, eat four small meals

Break the Sugar Addiction

When you eat healthy foods, it strengthens your body, immune system, and resilience. It changes how you look, think, and feel. It strengthens your energy, and energy equals health.

Sugar contradicts all of that. It will sap your energy and take you for a nosedive every time, just when you really need the energy. I've talked to so many people who say they have low energy or no energy. After ruling out medical issues, the way you eat is often the culprit. If you're hyped up on sugar, you won't have the endurance you need to get through the day.

Notable Facts about Sugar:

♦ Sugar increases the inflammation in your body and is highly acidic, which helps store fat and dump insulin into your blood. The more insulin you have in your blood throughout your lifetime, the less longevity you have. Try reducing your sugar with my cease and replace method.

♦ When you eat sugar, the body burns it for energy, but it also depletes your energy.

♦ Eating and burning healthy fats is key. They not only help you lose weight and keep you energized but they reduce your affinity for sugar.

♦ When you eat healthy fats, you will not crave sugar because these healthy fats suppress hunger, satiate you, and move your body away from burning sugar as your primary fuel source to burning fat instead.

♦ You could also be missing minerals if you are craving sugar.

Strength Conditioning

It's important to note that resilience is all about whole-body strengthening and firming. The strength moves I'm recommending are designed to give you an overall "360 workout," which means it will hit all major muscle groups. A good program includes cardio, core, work, flexibility, functional, and resistance training.

All the moves I'm recommending complement each other and balance out the body. Working muscles on one side of your body and then the other side of the body work together to improve posture, improve strength, and improve balance and stability.

Core strength, in particular, is important to single out because it is the center of the body and vital to function, longevity, and quality of life. Core strength becomes even more important as you age. A strong core stabilizes your entire body, giving you better balance and better posture. Performing core exercises as you age can also help prevent falls, decrease back pain, and allow you to maintain your independence for longer. When you build your core strength, you also make your body more resilient against other pressures and stressors of life.

Stay focused because some people get very fixated on the parts of their body they don't feel good about and work on only those parts. For example, they say things like, "I want to have muscular arms. I want to firm up my thighs. I want flat abs, etc." You may be one of those people too. I tell them, and I say to you, even if you do a million sit-ups, you won't get washboard abs. But if you focus on a holistic approach to working the entire body, you can get the results you want.

Fact: Spot reducing doesn't work.

Micro Moves to Strengthen Your Body

These micro moves will improve your strength, balance, core, and flexibility both physically and mentally. It's safe, it's effective, and it's never too late to start. Once you build them into your lifestyle, it will become effortless to maintain. Just like you brush your teeth or comb your hair, it can become a normal part of your daily routine.

Start by integrating one or two moves into your day from the list below. Keep working with those moves for about two to three weeks, or however long it takes for you to get comfortable with that habit. Then, move on to the next micro move. You may even want to do a circuit or a combination of moves together.

A Few Rules:

> ***Remember to check with your doctor before starting any exercise regimen.**

- ◆ Do the moves—one, five, or ten minutes at a time. The key is to start small and grow with it. Do a little each day and work on making it a habit.

- ◆ Start with two, five- or ten-minute walks. Try it during a two-minute commercial. Pick just one healthy habit to master before adopting another.

- ◆ The "no pain, no gain" thing? Just because you don't feel sore after today's workout doesn't mean it didn't do any good. Overcome any skepticism on thinking things like, "What's five minutes going to do?" Plenty. The objective is to ease into and develop a new lifelong habit. That is the best way to create resilience.

- ◆ Be your best you! A lot of people work out like crazy trying to mold their bodies to be like someone else, which is usually impossible.

You shouldn't go into any exercise program expecting to come out the other end looking like a celebrity. Many unhealthy behaviors result from trying to fit into a mold that's not you. It's important to focus on your process, at your pace, one micro step at a time to combat old beliefs.

Warm-Ups

Before you begin any activity—whether it's cardio, flexibility or strength moves—always prepare your mind and body by warming up.

Here's one example of a warm-up: Start out doing it for two minutes. March in place and roll your shoulders backward several times and then forward. Then open up into big arm circles like you're doing a back stroke in the pool. Then reverse that motion. Follow up with an overhead stretch.

Cardio Gives Your Heart and Mind Resilience

Cardio is cognitive training and vital for overall heart health, metabolism, and cerebral blood flow. Increasing your heart rate with regular endurance exercises (like listed below) can preserve existing brain cells and encourage new brain cell growth. Not only is exercise good for your body, it can also help to improve memory, increase focus, and sharpen your mind. Overall, cardio helps to develop a sense of self-worth and self-respect.

Choose a cardio routine that is most convenient and enjoyable. Again, start with one, two, five, or ten minutes—whatever you can handle.

- Walking
- Marching

- Running
- Biking
- Dancing
- Swimming
- Water aerobics
- Stair climbing

Flexibility Gives Your Spirit Fluidity and Resilience

Flexibility is essential but is often overlooked and always under-estimated when it comes to overall health. Regardless of age, you can improve your flexibility and overall mobility. It takes only a few minutes a day. These stretches can be done at any time of day. I like to fit them in while cooking, at the grocery store, waiting for gas, during TV commercials, first thing in the morning, before bed-time, or anytime I think about it.

Try some of these stretches as a daily part of your flexibility regimen:

- Downward-Facing Dog with chair
- Knee to Chest
- Seated Pigeon (Butt Stretch)
- Inner Thigh Stretch with Twist

Downward-Facing Dog with Chair

This stretches your shoulders, sides, and lower body.

How to do it:

1. Stand facing the back of a chair.

2. Place your hands lightly on the chair back and straighten your arms.

3. Hinging at your hips, take a few steps back so that your spine becomes parallel with the floor. Straighten your legs, lengthen your spine and keep it neutral from head to tailbone.

4. Push your chest through your arms toward the floor and hold here for three to five breaths of slow deep breathing.

5. Bend your knees, and take baby steps toward the chair, rounding your back slightly as you return to standing.

How Many: Hold the stretch for 20–30 seconds. Do 3–5 sets.

◆ **Make it easier:** Keep your knees soft or bend one knee at a time for a hip stretch.

◆ **Make it harder:** Place hands on the floor instead of a chair or place hands on a wall with your hands at hip height. Step back and push the wall away.

This is great to do in the morning to get your day started and, in the evening, before bed.

Knee to Chest

This is an excellent stretch for your glutes and back.

How to do it:

1. Sit tall in a chair with your feet on the floor and hips, knees, and toes facing forward.

2. Slowly inhale, and as you exhale, draw your right knee toward your chest, emptying all the air out of your lungs.

3. On your next inhale, lower your leg back to the starting position.

4. Exhale, drawing your left knee into your chest this time.

5. Continue alternating and hold the stretch for three to five breaths on each side.

How Many: Hold the stretch for 20–30 seconds. Do 3–5 sets daily.

◆ **Make it easier:** Do this while lying on your back on the floor or in bed.

◆ **Make it harder:** Do this in a standing position.

This is great to do in the morning to get your day started and in the evening before bed.

Seated Pigeon (Butt Stretch)

This stretch opens up your hips.

How to do it:

1. Sit tall in a chair with your feet on the floor and hips, knees, and toes facing forward.

2. Place your right ankle on top of your left knee.

3. Keep your right foot flexed, one hand on knee and the other on your ankle. Inhale.

4. As you exhale, hinge forward slightly at the hips, keep your butt rooted in the chair and hold with slow breaths.

5. Return to the starting position and repeat on the opposite side, placing your left foot on top of your right knee.

How Many: Hold the stretch for 20–30 seconds. Do 3–5 sets daily.

- ◆ **Make it easier:** Rather than bringing your foot to your opposite knee, cross your legs at the ankles or knees, and then hinge forward.

- ◆ **Make it harder:** Hinge forward a little more and press knee down for deeper stretch.

This is great to do in the morning to get your day started and, in the evening, before bed.

Inner Thigh Stretch

This stretch will improve flexibility and range of motion in your leg muscles, and it will ease muscle tension in your legs and groin.

How to do it:

1. Sit at edge of the chair and stretch your right leg out to the side with your toe pointing forward.

2. Lean slightly forward and to your right with your left hand overhead and hold.

3. Repeat on the left side.

How Many: Hold the stretch for 20–30 seconds. Do 3–5 sets daily.

♦ **Make it easier:** Do this movement by slightly leaning forward but not to the side and keep hands on hips instead of overhead.

♦ **Make it harder:** Do this without the chair. Stand and stretch leg to the side pushing booty back.

This is great to do in the morning to get your day started and in the evening before bed.

Strength Conditioning Gives Your Body Muscle, Power, and Resilience

When you improve your strength and function, you gain control and freedom over your life. Weight training builds strength, improves self-confidence, sharpens mental focus, and helps you to sleep better; it may also help to prevent dementia and other degenerative diseases as you age.

Work through some of these moves one at a time:

1. Push-Ups
2. Lateral Raises
3. Scaptions
4. Side Leg Raises

5. Rear Leg Raises

6. Criss-Cross Crunches

7. Reverse Fly

8. Sit Squats with Calf Raises

9. Seated Leg Lift—Core

10. Bridge—Core

11. Single Leg—Balance *(no photo – see description)*

12. Heel-to-toe Walk—Balance *(no photo – see description)*

Push-Ups

This strengthens chest muscles, shoulders, back of your arms, abdominals, the "wing" muscles directly under your armpit, and the calf.

How to do it:

1. Stand an arm's length in front of a wall.
2. Lean forward slightly and put your palms flat on the wall at the height and width of your shoulders.
3. Raise up on your toes and slowly bring your body toward the wall.
4. Gently push yourself back so your arms are straight.

How Many: Work up to doing 10–20 of these or whatever you can handle. Do 2–3 times weekly.

- ◆ **Make it easier:** Use the wall.
- ◆ **Make it harder:** Use kitchen counter or floor.

Try this right before you leave home to go to work or run errands.

Lateral Raises

Lateral raises build stronger, larger shoulders, gives increased shoulder mobility, and work the trapezius muscle in your upper back.

How to do it:

1. Stand with a dumbbell (or water bottle) in each hand, arms at your sides.

2. Keep your belly pulled in and knees slightly bent.

3. Raise the weights slowly out to your sides with palms facing forward until they reach shoulder height.

4. Lower the weights slowly to the starting position.

How Many: Work up to doing 3 sets of 10–20 reps, 3 times a week.

 ◆ **Make it easier:** Start this exercise with no weights or very low weights and focus on good form and posture throughout movement.

 ◆ **Make it harder:** Do this exercise standing on one leg and you get more of a core, balance, and stability challenge.

Try this while watching a TV program or at the end of your day.

Scaptions

Scaptions are focused on the rear muscles in your upper back that help keep strong posture, focus on proper scapular alignment, and aid in stabilizing the ball and socket of the shoulder joint. They also help strengthen the rotator cuff on the eccentric portion of the exercise, which is why it's important to control downward movement.

How to do it:

1. Before you begin, think about pulling your shoulder blades back and down.

2. Stand with a dumbbell (or water bottle) in each hand, arms at your sides, palms facing in.

3. Brace your core and slowly lift the dumbbells in front of your body at about a 45-degree angle.

4. Raise the weights until they're slightly above shoulder height.

5. Lower the weights slowly back down with control.

How Many: Work up to doing 3 sets of 10–20 reps, 3 times a week.

◆ **Make it easier:** Start this exercise with no weights or very low weights and focus on good form and posture throughout movement.

◆ **Make it harder:** Do this exercise standing on one leg, and you get more of a core, balance, and stability challenge.

Try this while watching a TV program or at the end of your day.

Side Leg Raises

This strengthens the glutes, hips, and thighs and can be done standing up or lying down on your side. This is also great for core, stability, and balance.

How to do it:

1. Stand next to a chair or wall and hold it for support.

2. Contract your abs and transfer your weight to your left leg.

3. Then lift your right leg out to the side as high as possible with toes facing forward.

4. Hold at the top of the raise, then slowly return to the starting position.

5. Repeat with your left leg.

How Many: Work up to doing 2–3 sets of 10–15 repetitions per leg every other day (or with a day's rest in between.)

- ◆ **Make it easier:** With support raise your leg only one foot high.

- ◆ **Make it harder:** Do this without holding on to anything. As you get stronger, add resistance with ankle weights, a resistance band, or cable machine.

You can sneak this in almost anywhere. Lying on the floor watching TV, waiting in line at the grocery store or post office.

Rear Leg Raises

This strengthens your lower back, glutes, and hamstrings
and can be done standing up or lying down on the stomach.
This is also great for core, stability, and balance.

How to do it:

1. Stand up tall and avoid bending forward.

2. Hold on to the back of a sturdy object like a chair or rest
   your hands on a wall and keep your core tight.

3. Raise one leg, pressing it straight back behind you, squeeze
   your glutes at the top of the motion, and pause (be careful
   not to hyperextend your back by raising your leg too high).

4. Return to the starting position.

How Many: Work up to doing 2–3 sets of 10–15 repetitions per leg every other day (or with a day's rest in between.)

- ◆ **Make it easier:** Raise your leg only one foot high.
- ◆ **Make it harder:** Do this without holding on to anything. As you get stronger, add resistance with ankle weights, a resistance band, or cable machine.

You can sneak this in almost anywhere. Lying on the floor watching TV, waiting in line at the grocery store or post office.

Criss-Cross Crunches
(Alternating Elbow-to-Knee Abdominals)

To help build your core, this strengthens the
abs, obliques, and hip flexors.

How to do it: You can do this standing, sitting, or lying down.

1. Put both hands behind your head, with elbows pointing outward.

2. Tighten your abdominal muscles.

3. Reach your right elbow to your left knee while exhaling.

4. If you're in a lying position, keep knees bent, with heels on the ground.

How Many: Work up to doing 2–3 sets of 10–30 reps.

◆ **Make it easier:** Use the sitting position if you are a beginner.

◆ **Make it harder:** Stand or lay on your back and use ankle weights

You can do this sitting or standing at the kitchen table right before you eat a meal.

Reverse Fly

Great for upper back and rear shoulder muscles.

How to do it:

1. Sit in a chair with feet shoulder-width apart, holding dumb-bells or water bottles at your sides.

2. Lean slightly forward, bringing your chest almost parallel to the floor.

3. Allow the weights to hang straight down, palms facing each other.

4. Maintain a tight core. Flatten your back and tighten your abs.

5. Exhale as you raise both arms out to your side, squeeze the shoulder blades together, and hold for 5–10 seconds.

6. Keep a soft bend in your elbows as you pull your shoulder blades toward the spine.

7. Inhale as you lower the weight back to the start position.

8. Avoid hunching your shoulders up during the movement.

9. Keep your chin tucked to maintain a neutral spine during the exercise.

10. Focus on feeling the shoulder blades coming together with proper breathing from start to finish.

How Many: Repeat for 8–12 repetitions. Do 3–5 sets, 3 times weekly.

- ◆ **Make it easier:** Do this movement with no weights and focus on proper form.

- ◆ **Make it harder:** Do this in a standing position. You may also lunge left to right while performing this exercise.

This is great to do in the morning to get your day started or in the evening before bed.

Sit Squats with Calf Raises

This sit-to-stand chair exercise is an excellent precursor to squats which strengthen leg and hip muscles. This will also help to gain or maintain the ability to get in and out of chairs independently, improving leg strength, functional balance, and control.

How to do it:

1. Start seated in a sturdy chair, feet planted on the floor about hip-distance apart.

2. Using as little assistance from hands or arms as possible, engage your core, and tip forward from the hips.

3. Press your weight through all four corners of your feet and push yourself to a standing position

4. Then raise up on your toes.

5. Reverse the movement, lowering heels to the floor, pressing your hips back, and bending your knees to carefully lower yourself to the seated position.

How Many: Work up to doing 2–3 sets of 10–30 reps, every other day.

 ◆ **Make it easier:** If you can't press all the way to a standing position, simply shift your weight forward, lift your glutes an inch or two from the chair seat, and hold for a second before lowering back down. Over time, work on developing the strength and balance necessary to come to a standing position.

 ◆ **Make it harder:** Do squats without using the chair; as you get stronger, do your squats while holding a weighted ball.

You can do this sitting in your office, on a park bench during your walk, or waiting for your car to be serviced.

Note: It's easy to take sitting and standing for granted as a fit, younger adult, but for some people, it can be a struggle to stand up from low chairs or soft couches.

Seated Leg Lift

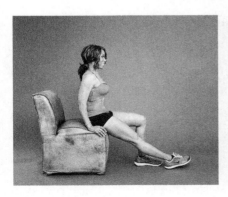 

This may look easy, but it works quite a few muscles. Core: strengthens abdominal muscles (rectus abdominis, transverse abdominis, internal and external obliques) and quadriceps.

How to do it:

1. Sit in a chair. Your left leg should be bent with your foot flat on the floor and your right leg extended.

2. Keep an upright posture; don't slouch or lean back in the chair.

3. Engage your core and raise your right leg.

4. Lift your leg as high as you can without letting your back collapse.

5. Circle your leg five times clockwise and five times counter-clockwise, and return your foot to the floor.

6. Repeat on the other side.

How Many: Do daily each move for 5–10 reps (per side).

◆ **Make it easier:** Do this exercise without circling leg. Instead, lift your leg off the floor and hold briefly before returning your foot to the floor.

◆ **Make it harder:** Do this exercise with ankle weights.

Do this anytime and anywhere you are sitting in a chair.

Bridges

This is great to mend low back pain. Core: glute bridges strengthen all three gluteal (butt) muscles—the maximus, medius, and minimus—in addition to your hamstrings and abductors.

How to do it:

1. Lie on your back with your hands along your sides, knees bent, both feet flat on the floor and at a comfortable distance from your butt.

2. Raise your hips until your body is in a straight line from your knee to your hip and to your shoulder.

3. Squeeze the glutes as tightly as you can in the top position while you hold for two seconds, and then lower back to the floor.

How Many: Work up to doing 3 sets of 10 reps, 3–4 times per week

◆ **Make it easier:** Do this exercise by holding in the raised hip position (isometric hold) for 10–15 seconds before lowering back to floor. Wait 15–30 seconds and repeat two more times to build strength.

◆ **Make it harder:** Use one leg instead of two. Lie on your back with your knees bent, one foot flat on the floor with the other hovering two inches off the floor.

Do this in the morning before or after you brush your teeth.

Single Limb Stance (Balance = Independence)

Challenging your balance is an essential part of a well-rounded exercise routine. It will give you more independence as you age.

Simply standing on one leg is an ability that everyone, young and old, should be able to perform but it's not easy for everyone. As we age, we lose musculoskeletal function, and neurological issues can impact balance, so strength is the key factor in standing on one foot.

How to do it:

1. Stand behind a steady, solid chair, and hold on to the back of it.

2. Lift up your right foot and balance on your left foot.

3. Hold that position for as long as you can, then switch feet.

4. Look straight ahead.

5. The goal is to stand on one foot without holding onto the chair and hold that pose for up to a minute.

How Many: Do 3 sets every day. Hold for 15 seconds and work your way up to 1 minute.

◆ **Make it harder:** Do this without a chair and instead of looking straight ahead, turn your head slowly from right to left and repeat. Also, try looking at the ceiling while holding your balance. This will challenge your neurological abilities too.

Do this daily anytime and anywhere. It's unlimited!

Walking Heel to Toe (Balance = Independence)

This exercise makes your legs stronger. It maintains an appropriate range of motion in your foot and ankle joints as well as adequate strength and stability within your muscles and ligaments. Better foot mechanics can lead to improved mechanics of the hips, knees, and core. Also, as you age, it enables you to walk without falling.

How to do it:

1. Put your right foot in front of your left foot so that the heel of your right foot touches the top of the toes of your left foot.

2. Move your left foot in front of your right, putting your weight on your heel.

3. Then, shift your weight to your toes.

4. Repeat the step with your left foot.

How Many: Take 20 steps a few times a day.

♦ **Make it easier:** Do this with a spotter (a person assisting you) or hold on to a stick for support so you don't fall. Start out by putting your right foot in front of your left foot, so the heel of your right foot touches the top of the toes of your left foot but don't walk—just hold that position for 10–20 seconds. Repeat this but change feet by putting your left foot in front of your right.

♦ **Make it harder:** Instead of looking forward when doing this exercise, turn your head to the right when you put your right foot in front of your left. When you put your left foot in front of your right, turn your head to the left. Then try the next round by looking at the ceiling as you walk forward.

♦ Also, try walking on your toes forward, then backward, by putting one foot in front of the other. This will challenge you neurologically, so you may want to do this with a spotter.

Do this anytime, anywhere, every day. It's unlimited!

Strength Thinking

Sharpening your mental strength is essential for reclaiming your strong and sexy. There is a cool bonus to that. It is said that a woman's biggest sex organ is her brain. Oh yeah! I can vouch for that! Using the brain first for anything should be the rule, not the exception.

So how do we age gracefully to reclaim our strong and sexy? Start with some mental strengthening exercises.

To increase mental strength, you need resilience training. That means you must choose courage over comfort because resilience training requires that you get familiar with being uncomfortable. This means you have to build up your tolerance for being uncomfortable—either mentally or physically.

Work Out Without Distractions

Working out is a great way to boost your physical and mental strength. If you're just starting to work out, find music, watch TV, or anything that will hype and psych you up for getting it done. The goal is to develop a consistent and flowing habit.

One way to build your tolerance for being uncomfortable is to work out without music, TV, phones, or social media and be present with your discomfort. Also, pay close attention to your breath and physical sensations.

Wait It Out When You're Hungry

Allow yourself to feel hunger pangs by waiting an extra five or ten minutes without grabbing a snack on impulse when you're hungry. Yes, you'll be uncomfortable, but that's the idea—for you to build your tolerance for more difficult challenges.

Talk to Someone

It can help you develop mental strength and become better. It will give you a different perspective. Start with your doctor to rule out physical health problems; then talk to a close friend, family member, or therapist. There's a big difference between "being strong" and "acting tough." Acting tough is about pretending you have no problems. Being strong is about admitting you don't have all the answers.

Practice Gratitude

Grateful people enjoy a host of benefits, such as a boost in immunity, better quality sleep, and more mental strength. Make thinking about what you appreciate a habit—either do it before you get out of bed in the morning or before going to sleep. Finding the silver lining shapes how we think about the world and is a big part of becoming stronger mentally.

Take a Cold Shower

Taking a cold shower in the morning doesn't just help the skin to retain moisture; it also gets your immune system and metabolism going for the day!

Taking a cold shower will boost your endocrine function and lymph circulation, which will boost your immune system and blood circulation. It also brings blood to the capillaries, strengthens the nervous system, and builds mental strength. It will provide ongoing physical and mental resilience training and give you a boost of endorphins and energy for the day.

Do Something You Don't Want to Do for Five or Ten Minutes

When there's something you really don't want to do, like a workout or tackling a boring report, tell yourself you only have to do it for ten minutes. When the ten-minute mark rolls around, permit yourself to quit if you want to. You're likely to keep going; starting is usually the hardest part.

Starting something you don't want to do trains your brain to know that you don't have to respond to how you feel. Just because you don't feel like doing it doesn't mean you can't do it. You're stronger than you think! You can take action even when you're not motivated.

This applies to taking on more significant challenges, too. When your brain tries to talk you out of doing something (like giving a presentation or trying a new hobby), respond with, *"Challenge Accepted!"*

Your brain underestimates you. But every time you do something that you thought you couldn't do, you challenge your brain to see you as more capable and competent than it gives you credit for.

Try New Things

Have you ever watched the wonder and excitement in a child's eyes as they try new things? It's beautiful. Each year as we age, that wonder in the eyes fades like a candle burning low. Stay up to date and relevant. Things are changing all the time. Staying up to date keeps you personally in the know and able to communicate more effectively with friends and family, so you don't feel old and like an outsider. Trying new things will encourage you to live longer and be a part of the continued fight to make a positive impact in the world.

Try Old Things

Don't get stuck in old, comfortable, rigid ways. Having said that, don't be afraid to revisit the good old times. Don't be embarrassed to go back and enjoy those things that made you feel good but other people shamed you out of liking as you got older. Some of the most miserable adults seem to have been taught that anything that's fun is not adult-like. Are adults only allowed to be miserable? You know what—if you want to sit in front of the television and watch the Saturday morning cartoons that you liked when you were a kid, go ahead!

Other Ways to Train Your Brain

Give your brain a daily workout to sharpen your focus and preserve existing brain cells:

- Engage in stimulating conversation
- Learn a foreign language
- Take online courses
- Give your brain a break (with meditation or breathing exercises)
- Work on a hobby
- Look, listen, learn

Best Foods for Your Brain

- Fatty fish
- Fruits
- Leafy greens
- Nuts
- Pumpkin seeds
- Tea and coffee
- Turmeric

◆ Whole grains—whole grains such as bread, pasta, barley, brown rice, oatmeal, and bulgur wheat contain vitamin E, which is used to protect and preserve healthy cells.

Micro Moves for a Healthier Life

◆ **Practice micro resilience with your food and exercise—** Micro resilience is when you tell yourself that you really want that piece of cake, but you'll wait an hour before you eat it. If you still want it, you can have it, but wait an hour first. Likely, you won't care anymore, and you will totally forget.

◆ **Pacify yourself with your favorite blankie—**It could be a massage, a favorite movie, or just curling up by the fireplace—whatever makes you feel good. Your pacifier should not be food.

◆ **Surround yourself with like-minded people who want to do the same—**When you do what you love in life and surround yourself with positive people you love, you maximize your joy.

◆ **Sleep well—**Sleep deprivation is the cause of many accidents and diseases. The body needs recovery. It needs to recharge itself to think, create, and function properly. Rhythmic breathing (inhale for four and hold for sixteen, exhale for eight) or counting backward by three is helpful.

◆ **Supplementation—**Get a yearly blood test to know what you need.

◆ **Hydration—**Get in at least sixty-four ounces daily. This is just an estimate. That can change depending on weight, gender, and activities. It's so simple but effective. The power of it is widely underestimated. Dehydration is the root of many deaths and things going sideways in life.

◆ **Don't believe the hype**—Shut down and shut out media news that shoves down your throat how you can be an overnight success. No such thing!

PART FOUR

Refine

WENDY'S WISDOM:

*If you live in a cell of shame, secrecy,
and fear, you can never be free.*

CHAPTER 9

Forgiveness and Skeletons

"Watch your thoughts, they become your words; watch your words, they become your actions; watch your actions, they become your habits; watch your habits, they become your character; watch your character, it becomes your destiny."

—Lao Tzu

Many years after leaving New Jersey, I knew I had come a long way. Trophies decorated my home, and I could proudly say that I had broken world records. But not everything was peachy keen. Privately, I still had demons that haunted me by day and came alive at night in my dreams. They stopped me from doing things I wanted to do. I even sabotaged some opportunities that could have changed my life because the demons said I couldn't do any more than I'd done. Old messages and stories that were fed to me in the past rose up in my mind, dragging me back down to a place I didn't want to revisit.

I suffered in silence, but I wasn't exactly alone. I sat with the skeletons of my past, which had only been illuminated when I made it through dark Hallways. I wasn't running for my life or processing the trauma that I had just survived, so I could sit back and see everything that had led to that moment.

As I examined the skeletons in my life, I saw those disparaging messages for what they really were. I realized that ideas were pushed on me to make certain choices and think certain things, none of which were helpful or true. I didn't consider what other choices I could have made until I was able to sit and reflect.

During that time of reflection, I learned a lot and gained a wider perspective. When I examined everything that had led to the trauma in my life, I realized I could prevent it from happening again. I recognized what I had been conditioned to believe, what people programmed me to believe, and realized that the choices I saw other people make weren't the only possibilities. That's when I was able to give myself the opportunity to write my own rules and keep from getting in that bad place again.

To live life fully, you have to get to the root of things that drain your courage and stop you from achieving your goals and dreams. You have to face the things that keep you living in fear with deep, dark secrets and generational curses. Once you face these things, you won't have to live life speaking in a whisper. You can jump for joy, cheer, dance, and do all of the things you have ever dreamed of doing in your life!

Your preparation up to this point by working on the mental and physical aspects from previous chapters should give you the fortitude and strength you need to feel safe enough to move forward. If you don't feel ready, just go back and rework those chapters again.

How Do We Get to Understand That This Is Bigger than Us?

How do we become a game-changer instead of a problem collector? Sometimes what happens to us is not our fault. We may have had a bad upbringing or received bad personal advice from someone we trusted. Maybe we were tainted due to generational curses (repeated patterns) that we were born into.

You can use your wisdom, experience, and intuition to break the cycle.

Start by investigating your history. Look for patterns and stories about intergenerational trauma. Ask questions like:

- What conditioned me to think or react a certain way?
- How did I get here?
- What factors made me accept those outcomes?
- Why did I think certain choices were okay?
- How do I fix this so I don't do it again?

When you have answers, you will be less likely to repeat your past mistakes, and it will keep you moving forward instead of backward. Moving forward requires resilience, gratitude, and more.

The most significant skeletons hiding behind our trauma are deep within us, but we have to face them so we don't repeat mistakes and end up back in the Hallways that we have just exited. Once we face these skeletons, we have more room to create new, positive behaviors.

Whether you acknowledge them or not, these skeletons are a sign that something needs to be aligned. To gain resilience, you must assess and resolve the issues you have experienced—hurts, disagreements, regret, discouragement, anger—otherwise, you can become a "problem collector," which is too much of a burden to bear for anyone.

So, the question is where can you find these skeletons? They're in a place I call the Safe Box. How can you find protection when you begin chasing them? That's the place I call the Safe Space.

The Safe Space

The Safe Space is a place in your mind where you can go to be comforted when you feel yourself falling apart. Think of it as an important "time out" for yourself.

Creating your Safe Space requires you to sit down and think about a place that immediately makes you feel better—it can be real or imagined. Go there when you feel you are going to have a meltdown. I have several places that give me peace. For example, I've created a Safe Space on a dock in Jamaica. That's one of my happy vacation spots; it makes me smile. Another is on a lakefront in Ateronda (that's my pretend place). It's calm and sedate, and I'm surrounded by nature, birds, and water. When the world is too much, I can go to this dock and feel safe. In this Safe Space, I practice gratitude and self-care. A new part of you can be born through this process.

The Safe Box

The Safe Box is a receptacle containing the overflow of trauma from our past. It represents the pain and fear (past skeletons) with an intense impact on our lives with no resolution. The Safe Box is where you shoved all the things that happened to you that you couldn't deal with when they occurred because you either didn't have time right then or you couldn't afford to break down. Even years later, you may not want to confront those issues because you're afraid you can't handle them. But the truth is those boxed-up skeletons are quietly eating away at you and rotting you from the inside out.

These things cause you to shut down to protect yourself. But here's what happens when you do that. It chokes off your personality and all of those great and special qualities about you—the things that make you YOU!

Steamer Trunk

Picture the Safe Box as a lockbox or locked treasure chest in which you have been stuffing things for years.

I remember when I first realized how much I had stuffed in my Safe Box. It felt like the weight of the world was on me. I was achieving things, but something was still holding me back.

It felt like I was dragging a big suitcase like a steamer trunk, and it was filled with old trauma. It made it harder to climb out of the hole I was in, but I still managed. I was dragging this big trunk, and I didn't know why I was hauling it around. It had always been with me—it had become a part of me, in fact.

But each time I would get closer to the top, I realized how much harder this steamer trunk was making every move. So, I had to think . . . what is the steamer trunk doing for me? Then I realized—it was just holding me back.

That's when I asked, for the first time, what was in the steamer trunk and whether I still needed anything inside. As it turned out, inside was all the crap from my life I hadn't dealt with, like problem parents, abuse, bullying, etc. I had shoved it all down to survive. But because I did my work in the Hallway, now I had a different perspective; as a result, I knew I didn't want to drag those old hurts around anymore.

When we collect all that trauma and stuff it in a Safe Box, it builds and builds. Eventually, the box breaks open in extremely negative ways that don't serve you well, which can create problems. We think the trauma has been locked away, but it's not really gone. We know it's still there, even when we do our best to ignore those feelings. We end up feeling diminished and bad about ourselves. We swallow our feelings because we're afraid to confront the trauma in the box, and the trauma becomes a part of us which we act out in every aspect of our lives.

Whether it's a spouse who was unfaithful, a parent who let you down as a child, or a friend who shared something you told them in confidence, we all have some forgiving to do. Everyone has a past, and most of us have skeletons that haunt us. We all have things in our past that we would like to do differently. Unfortunately, the past cannot be changed, forgotten, edited, erased, or auctioned off. BUT you do have choices! You can choose your response to past traumas and pick one that empowers your life instead of destroying it.

Don't Bottle It Up!

Bottled-up trauma can cause nervousness, stress, overeating, weight gain, energy loss, clinical depression, and more. It affects how you communicate, what you eat, how you react, sleep, walk, and talk, and the energy you bring to the table when you meet people. It affects everything!

And the worse part? When you've lived with the pain and torture of an acknowledged trauma long enough, you may not remember what normal is supposed to feel like. You might not even know or remember how the trauma started, but left unchecked, it will gradually destroy your body and your spirit and diminish your quality of life.

That is exactly what happened to a client of mine. Her name was Gail. She was harboring a lot of anger. She said she wanted to lose weight, but I knew something was holding her back. So, I spent more time on life coaching than I did weight training and physical exercise. Her past hurts affected everything she did, and they were holding her back from succeeding with her overall health and body goals. Every time she would get close to reaching her goals, she would self-sabotage.

Nothing I did or said could convince her to let go of her past and anger. I even took her to a spiritual healer and a psychologist. She shut them down. She just couldn't let her past go. Unfortunately, she developed cancer which I believe came at least in part from all those years of repressed hurt and anger. She died young at age fifty-one.

That's one of the reasons I do my best to consider my clients' complete lifestyle—physical and emotional. You cannot get into the ring and just work your body, ignoring the rest of what's going on in your life and expect to achieve any long-term success.

When you nurture the whole person, you gain resilience. When you confront and conquer your fears, you gain resilience. When you open the Safe Box under your own terms and handle the skeletons inside, that is proof you are gaining resilience. That is how I have been able to unpack my pain and gain the strength to change my future.

Unpacking Your Pain

How do you find the resilience to carefully open the Safe Box and look inside? How do you navigate the old burdens of secrecy and shame you were taught to feel about what happened? And most importantly, how do you make peace with the memories that aren't good?

Understand What Is in Your Safe Box!

As I've said, we all have shared trauma due to what we've survived during the COVID pandemic, and that trauma is not going to magically disappear just because restaurants have opened up. We can pretend it's gone, but we have just put it in our Safe Box. We are changed forever!

Experiencing trauma, no matter what kind, has a physiological effect that leaves an imprint on your body and your mind. The fearful expectations and unhealthy coping mechanisms can be passed down through history. Again, if something happened to your grandparent and they never dealt with it, their responses (which were shaped by the trauma they experienced) affected your parents. If they never confronted that damage and worked through it, that inherited trauma also affected you. Breaking that cycle of trauma affecting your body is essential; it stops generational curses and creates a better world for your children and their children.

As I've said before, intergenerational trauma is more extensive than one person or one family. Systemic racism, misogyny, homophobia, and xenophobia are baked into our culture, and they take a toll. Because the system itself perpetuates these negative views, which drive damaging actions and policies, some of the good choices have been intentionally placed where they are much harder to reach. Mistakes are punished more severely, with second chances harder to get for people who fall into the groups that are discriminated against.

The cultural myth tells us that anyone can be anything if they just work hard enough, which doesn't take those obstacles into account. That feeds feelings of shame and guilt and inadequacy for "failing." Even worse, we can internalize negative views about ourselves from that toxic societal narrative, from what we were taught or what we pick up from the culture around us.

Our parents may have accepted those damaging ideas as "the way the world works" without question or research. Or maybe, faced with what seemed like insurmountable odds, they just gave up and taught you to think small in a misguided attempt to protect you from disappointment.

These wounds and restrictions pile up from generation to generation, getting passed on by word and example. We can feel rage over the unfairness and lack of progress and feel hopeless. When those emotions turn inward instead of finding healthy ways to express and work through them, they eat us alive in the form of depression, unhealthy coping mechanisms, and physical illness like high blood pressure.

In other words, you, your parents, and your forebears made the choices that you understood were available, even though the ones society served up were limited and damaged. When you realize that society is corrupt in many ways and has been engineered to feed people lies to keep them limited, you see a broader horizon with all the choices, opportunities, and possibilities that exist but weren't presented to you. Now you can do better because you have better information.

If you have lost weight, gained weight, or changed your appearance during the pandemic, know that the reasons go beyond your diet and exercise. If you are not physically where you want to be, know that the cause might lie in your Safe Box. Don't be ashamed. You can still get back on track, reroute, and get to the place—mentally and physically—you want to be. Stop beating yourself up.

Instead, release the stress and accept where you are with your body right now. Understand where you are and believe that you will be okay. It doesn't always feel like it, especially when things are going wrong or when you are faced with a difficult situation or challenge. But you have the opportunity to see these challenges and situations as an opportunity to grow and become even better than you know. You need to trust yourself and keep the faith that you are strong enough and capable of getting through *anything*!

One Thing at a Time

Shift your mindset before you try to unpack even one skeleton from your Safe Box. Go to your Safe Space first. Find your courage, put on your big kid pants, and declare out loud and in writing that *you are breaking the chain*. Write it down! Say it to a friend, family member, or therapist! Let this micro move begin your new life by confronting your skeletons and consciously making different decisions to change history from this day on.

Cleaning out the skeletons are necessary to heal, but you have to do so carefully. Don't open and dump the box all at once. Allow yourself to continue to make micro moves, especially initially. "Go big or go home" doesn't work here either when you're sifting through the Safe Box. Take out one thing at a time. Assessing and resolving everything within the Safe Box at once is too much of a burden for anyone.

It's important to remember *why* you are unpacking your box. Your goal is to release the past so you can show up for the present.

You will find questions of worthiness and self-esteem. Once you clean out the box, you will understand that you were born worthy or you wouldn't be here, and you deserve your best life—the life you have imagined in your Safe Space.

Some people keep their Safe Box hidden away even though they know how dangerous it is. They don't feel strong enough to open up what's inside. They lack confidence or experience fear. So where can you begin? Commit to mastering only one micro move at a time.

Change Your Perspective

How are you picturing your Safe Box right now? The way you picture your Safe Box in your mind will determine how you unpack it. The Safe Box can feel like a scary basement that's dark and creepy. If that's how you imagine it, turn on all the lights and change your image of the Safe Box to be something more controllable and not scary. Things don't look as scary in the light.

If your Safe Box looks like a big, ominous, dark trunk, change it up! Make it a flower-covered suitcase or cover the box with your favorite pattern. I love glitter and bright colors, so I cover my box in those. Picturing the Safe Box in this way gives me energy, makes me happy, and motivates me. But you need to do what works for you.

Make the Safe Box as ridiculous or as exciting as you want. Picture anything other than darkness. The mind is a powerful thing; when you change how you think about unpacking your trauma, you've already won half the battle.

Switch the Focus

When you change your perspective, you might find yourself more willing to forgive other people. What happens to us is not always the fault of other people in our lives. They are also carrying a Safe Box of generational curses and trauma.

Focusing your energy on wishing bad luck or other evils on people who hurt you is like trying to push them into a ditch. You fall in with them. You attract whatever you think about most often, even when intended for someone else. So be careful not to attract blame, whether it's directed at yourself or others.

You can't blame the people who didn't know how to unpack their Safe Box. And you certainly can't blame yourself. Be sincere about forgiving whatever happened to you and release it. Let it go. Forgiving doesn't mean letting yourself be hurt by that person again or contacting them—and it doesn't mean taking them back into your life if they've shown no remorse. Forgiveness heals you by untangling you from the chains that hold you to the past.

Don't waste your energy on things you can't control and things that won't benefit you in the future. Release your fears. Release your limiting beliefs and release that part of you that felt shame. Now pat yourself on the back and reward yourself with praise for doing that.

Focus on the skills you've learned here to break the cycle instead of wasting your energy living in regret, trying to seek revenge, or holding onto a grudge. Life is too short.

Rather than seeking revenge on someone, seek wisdom for yourself so you don't fall victim the next time you encounter a similar situation. Develop a "warrior" mindset, one that believes that vengeance is not your job—it's the Lord's.

Pushing Past Fear Out of the Victim Role

Think of fear as a serious disease (because it is), and you need to nurse yourself back to health. Fear affects every part of your life. It immobilizes you and is a major factor leading to depression. Fear breaks you down, and it will keep you feeling like a victim if you let it. Remember—you have a choice. Refuse to let fear win.

To push past fear and escape from a victim mentality, you must be honest with yourself. Name it and claim it! Ask yourself, "What am I afraid of—and why?" Once you have faced your fear and know what it is, you can own it, which gives you the power to break its hold on you.

Fear is often born from the emotional baggage, secrecy, and shame surrounding those skeletons in your Safe Box. Maybe you fear being hurt again, making the same mistakes, or being judged. Some people fear success, being alone, or not being good enough. And let's not forget the fear of COVID. You've been afraid for so long that fear has become a part of you. It's made you feel insecure, unsure, and inadequate about making the right choices. But you can change that right now.

What you have learned in the previous chapters will help you build new strength. Review the lessons often to reinforce a new habit that will help you build the courage to push through your fears and gain resilience.

Try these steps when things get intense.

1. **Visualize.** Create a scene in your head of the actual situation you need to push through. Imagine yourself handling the problem successfully. Then see and feel the benefits that came from that experience.

2. **Breathe.** In the midst of panic or anxiety, try this rhythmic pattern to regain control and clear your head. Inhale for a count of four, hold for a count of twelve, and exhale for a count of eight. Repeat the pattern five to ten times or until your heart stops racing and your mind clears.

3. **Get Support.** Have a trusted friend, mentor, coach, or therapist keep you accountable for pushing through your fears.

4. **Go to Your Safe Space.** Give yourself permission to take a breath and take a break by retreating to your Safe Space for some rest and recovery.

Keep in mind that fear isn't always as straightforward as you may think. Fear is not just running from a big, scary monster or going through a haunted house. Fear also manifests itself in procrastination, excuses, and perfectionism. Those are all stalling tricks to keep from doing what scares you. So, if you are procrastinating, making excuses, or trying to achieve perfection before proceeding with a business project, health issues, even making a phone call, or anything at all, you are reacting out of fear.

Make a conscious shift now to push past that fear, and your life will instantly change! Identify what you're afraid of. Take responsibility for managing your fear. Then move forward. Make sure to celebrate your success along the way. Baby steps count!

Forgiving Yourself through a "Spirit Self-Search"

There comes a point when you must decide whether you are willing to forgive and, if so, how to start that process. Forgiveness begins by making a different choice. Sometimes you just have to accept that you will never get an apology from the person who hurt you. In other cases, your best interests may lie with turning the other cheek and being the bigger person, regardless of what's happened to you. That doesn't mean you should turn your back! You are not required to give someone a chance to hurt you again. Forgive—but don't make yourself vulnerable.

When you forgive those who hurt you, two things happen. You find a sense of peace, and you take away their power. They have power over you as long as you dwell on the memories of the harm done. Their power is in your hurting heart and soul until you dig into your Safe Box and release those skeletons. Hate and anger sap your self-worth. When you release those feelings, you now have room to welcome peace and a brighter future. In the future, you can rebuild and strengthen your mind, body, spirit, and resilience.

It's also important to note that you:

◆ Don't need to understand why other people did what they did. Just know that they acted from limited thinking, misinformed beliefs, and their own unsealed traumas. Most of the time, when we unintentionally hurt someone, we act from limited thinking.

◆ Don't play the blame game. Stop holding others responsible for your inner distress. No one has the power to make you miserable without your consent.

While you're on the path of not blaming others for your feelings, remember that you can't blame yourself either! You want to forgive those who insulted you, attacked you, or took you for granted. But remember more than anything, you must forgive yourself first.

Forgive yourself for what? For how you blame yourself for "allowing" people to hurt you. If someone took advantage of you as a child or used their power over you to cause harm, you are not to blame. If you were manipulated, lied to, or misused because you were trusting, innocent, or naive, that is not your fault. If someone you had every reason to rely on betrayed your trust—a parent, older relative, authority figure, or close friend—that is on them, not you.

Did you make a bad choice in the past that put you in a situation to get hurt? Realize that you did the best you could with the knowledge and maturity you had at the time. Maybe you didn't have complete information, or other people pressured you, or you didn't stop to think things through. Perhaps you were sick or in pain and not able to think clearly. Once you figure out what contributed to making a poor choice, now you know what *not* to do next time so you can avoid repeating the mistake!

Until you stop mourning the past and blaming yourself, you won't be able to progress. Let go. It's not too late to make a fresh start!

Because writing is therapeutic for me, it's no surprise that working on this book made me reflect on my memories and unpack more pain from my past. I find myself in some of the same life predicaments that I remember my mother being in, and it really hurts to realize how much I took her for granted.

It hurts that I wasn't there for her before her early death at forty-two. But I forgive myself for not being mature enough to know what to do back then. And I forgive myself for not knowing what I didn't know and couldn't have known at the time. I treasure the strong woman she was and how she taught me to be strong in so many little ways. Today, I understand why she made some of the decisions she made, and I respect her fully for doing the best she could. I am grateful for the time we shared before her death, and I am grateful that I can still share and hug her in my memories and give her the praise she deserves when I meet with her in my Safe Space. Hold on . . . I think I need to go there right now!

It's Not an Overnight Flight

Although it can sometimes feel impossible, the process of forgiving yourself means letting go of old grievances and judgments. You must allow yourself to heal. By forgiving yourself, you are accepting the reality of what happened to you and finding a way to live in a state of resolution. This is not an overnight change. It's a gradual process, but you become stronger and more resilient once you do this. Things really do get better.

Let me warn you about one important thing before you decide to make amends. Do not attempt to forgive yourself, or anyone else for that matter, unless you have fully identified, felt, expressed, and released your anger and pain.

If you find at first that you are unwilling to forgive, search your mind and spirit to determine why. Ask yourself questions like:

- ◆ Are you addicted to feeling that angry adrenaline?

- ◆ Are you filled with thoughts of revenge?

- ◆ Do you feel powerless? Some people truly have been victimized. Recognizing that they were preyed upon can be part of letting go of their self-blame. In that case, it's important not to get stuck in being a victim but to move towards being a survivor and then to becoming an advocate to help others.

- ◆ Do you like feeling self-righteous? It's tempting to hang onto anger and hurt because martyrdom makes you feel superior and self-righteous, a way to distract yourself from the pain. By playing the long-suffering martyr, you make yourself the hero of the story, but you also can't let go of the damage and be happy or you'll lose your special role. It's like catching a tiger by the tail—once you've caught him, you don't dare let go or you'll get eaten!

♦ Are you afraid that you must reconnect or you'll lose your ties to them?

I remember feeling some of these feelings when I was in a bad place. I didn't want to let go because I wasn't sure what would be left if I did, and I was afraid of feeling empty. I went from being afraid to feeling sorry for myself. After I felt and expressed my pain, anger, and grief, I was finally able to take control and let go of the negative feelings that were holding me hostage and turning my life upside down.

Negative energy is real! It will eat you up. When you identify and resolve your issues, you can move on.

Mental Tricks

Here's an important mental trick that really helps. In your imagination, pretend you're observing the situation as an outsider. Recognize the actions of the other person that hurt you. Acknowledge that it was wrong for them to do so.

Separate that acknowledgment from making judgments about why they did what they did. Yes, they might be a bad person, jealous, spiteful, or many other things. Or maybe they were acting out of their own woundedness, limited information, misunderstanding, or inability to see other choices.

You will probably never know why they hurt you. Even if you asked, they might not be able to tell you because they don't understand it themselves. If you can shift into feeling compassion for them like a hurt animal who bites and claws out of fear or pain, you can move away from needing to judge them and wish them healing.

When you stop needing to validate your feelings by judging the person who hurt you and feel compassion for the pain that caused their actions, you gain distance and perspective, which leads to inner peace. You'll feel happier and free of the negative energy of resentment. The bonus? You'll find that others are much more attracted to you. A peaceful person attracts peaceful energy.

Once you decide you are willing to forgive yourself, here's what to do:

- **First, become more familiar** with yourself, your thoughts and feelings, and your boundaries and needs.

- **Acknowledge the reality of what occurred** and how you were affected. Don't feel guilty because someone mistreated you. Trusting someone who should have done right by you doesn't make you weak. The fault is theirs, not yours.

- **Acknowledge the growth you experienced** because of what happened. What did it make you learn about yourself?

- **Find a quiet place** and uninterrupted time to be alone with your thoughts and be at one with yourself for a moment.

- **Shift your mental energy** to allow yourself to feel whatever emotions come up without needing to run away or push them down.

- **Refocus.** If you made poor choices that contributed to your pain, think about what you've learned so you can do things differently in the future. Release blame for not knowing what you didn't know.

- **Express forgiveness for yourself.** Say it out loud: "I for-give me!"

- **Give yourself a good talking to.** Say to yourself, "Self, this is a new day. I am willing to create a new and brighter chapter in my life. I forgive you! I forgive you! I forgive you!" Then, let it go for good! Feel it cleanse your soul. Say these words aloud with conviction and add as much explanation as you need to get the point through to your-self. Repeat it for at least seven days, two times a day: in the morning when you rise and in the evening before you sleep.

Feel to Heal

When I was told to try therapy, I foolishly resisted. I thought I was better than that. I thought asking for help was shameful, and I didn't want to be labeled as "crazy" (as I had heard people say). But my nightmares and screams in the night wouldn't stop, so I gave it a try.

I discovered that I had stuffed much more into my Safe Box than I first thought, both for things I felt ashamed of and things that were done to me that made me feel hurt, angry, and humiliated. It was locked deep inside my soul and I had thrown away the key because I didn't want to deal with it. I was afraid that dealing with all that would be too exhausting.

I'll admit, it knocked some of the wind out of me, but I'm so glad I finally did the work. It helped me achieve my dreams, freed my soul, and improved my health.

One of the first things I was told in therapy was to for-give everything and everybody. That was difficult. Since I wasn't a hundred percent invested in the idea, I mechanically mouthed the words "I forgive you" to my ex. I didn't really mean it, but I thought saying it would satisfy the homework I was given and magically make everything better. I knew it was fake, and it backfired on me. I became angrier. I thought I'd never get rid of my problems and my nightmares would never end. I continued to suffer in silence until I meant what I said and made my peace with God. It wasn't until I recognized this that I truly broke the cycle of fear-based thinking.

Trusting yourself and trusting the process is essential. You have to feel to heal, and you have to put in the work and mean it. I tried faking the process, but really, I faked out myself instead.

Be authentic and grab deep down in your soul. Mean what you say and say what you mean, so you don't prolong your suffering like I did.

Forgive those who hurt you, forgive the things that happened to you, and forgive yourself. Forgiveness is one of the greatest gifts you can give yourself. The power lies within you. Make the choice to look inside and find it.

Micro Tools for Unpacking Your Safe Box

It's essential to dig deep and get to the root of things so you don't fall into the same old patterns that filled up your Safe Box in the first place. Confronting old hurts and working through past trauma is challenging but essential. Doing the work will keep you moving forward and help you create new, more positive behaviors.

Just remember, we must feel to heal to gain resilience. Practicing gratitude and self-care, along with acknowledging the wins and celebrating the progress you've already made, will help you avoid falling back into old, less effective coping mechanisms.

The micro tools I'm going to share will help you keep your Safe Space sacred, but they will also help you open your Safe Box, little by little, and be empowered by it instead of overwhelmed.

Call Up Your Safe Image in Your Safe Space When the World Gets Too Scary

Call up your mental Safe Space with five slow, deep breaths. Think of one thing right now that you are grateful for. Envision someone who showed you love who has passed on. Think about the happy memories you shared with them. Play those visions repeatedly in your mind and let them fill you with joy. Wrap your arms around your own body for a big virtual hug from them and let yourself really feel it. Know that you can visit that place any time you want joy, love, and safety.

I visualize virtual hugs often or whenever I need them, and it is very soothing for me. When I'm in my Safe Space, it's my world and I'm in control. I choose whether I go or stay and for how long. Finding my Safe Space is so liberating and soothing, and I feel so much gratitude in this state because I am open and willing to be vulnerable.

That creates great energy and a wonderful start to my day, which makes me feel loved no matter how crazy and noisy the world gets. Going to my Safe Space and opening myself to deeper understanding strengthens and empowers me with love and gratitude deep within my soul. It gives me the courage to continue the fight, push past my fears, and reach for everything I desire. What I do in my Safe Space grounds me for the whole day.

Write a Letter

If you're still struggling to release your pain and anger, writing a letter to those who hurt you is a good way to get everything out and into the open. It works whether those people are living or deceased.

Get all of your frustrations out on paper. Say everything plainly and really mean it, but come from the pain point, not the blame point. This micro move is all about you and how you feel and what's occurred in your life more than it is about demanding an apology or wanting to shame or punish them. It's about taking responsibility for your future by owning your past so you can move on and learn from it to make things better.

If the person who hurt you is still living, consider giving that letter to them or mailing it if you feel sure that doing so won't spark safety concerns. If you are worried about possible retribution, realize that just the process of writing the letter is therapeutic because you got to say your piece.

If you do share your letter, try not to have expectations about the outcome. Consider how you might feel if you are rebuffed or if no apology is forthcoming—both of which are, unfortunately, possibilities. If those scenarios are too anxiety-producing, tuck the letter away and revisit your choices in the future.

Decide in advance what to do if the person wants a phone call or in-person conversation. Will you feel safe doing so? Set boundaries, so you avoid physical danger. Do you believe the request is being made sincerely, or does the other person want to continue the fight? You are under no obligation to allow someone to verbally or emotionally abuse you in the name of "hearing their side."

If the person is deceased, burn your letter or store it. Then go to a room, shut the door, and shout your feelings to the universe.

The point of this exercise is to expel the hurt from your soul, wash the pain from your consciousness, and come to terms with the anger and disappointment. It works—I can testify to that.

This was another part of my process to avoid staying stuck in the past. I needed to release my hurt and unburden my hardened heart. Only then was I able to let love in again. Only then was I willing to become vulnerable, yet strong enough, to give away my precious prize—my heart.

Don't let your past rule your future. Don't let it control how you act, what you eat, how you speak, how you feel, or what you do daily.

Let Go of Grudges and Animosity

Grudges are infections that slowly eat away at your soul and cut your life short. Life's too short to waste on things that don't matter and things you can't control. Picture what's bothering you as a helium balloon and let it go, watching it float away in the air. Detox from revenge fantasies and use that energy on positive actions that will help you grow, improve your coping skills, and increase your confidence.

CHAPTER 10

Soaring Above the Rest

The Promise

Once you've had some healing, then it's time for growth.
If you want to live your best life, you must do both.

As you begin your journey things might not make sense,
but soon you'll find meaning and purpose with lots of confidence.

So, push past your fears and wipe away your tears,
but never back down and you'll find wisdom beyond your years.

Awaiting you is everything you desire,
you just have to get out there and put your feet to the fire!

With all your grace, gifts, skills, and charm,
every dream you've dreamed, you can achieve without harm.

And if you should falter and have doubt or concern,
know that sometimes you win, but sometimes you just learn.

Have faith that you can do it.
Building strength will get you through it.
And as long as you never give up, guaranteed you will do it . . . Promise!

Take a deep breath! You've been healing. And now that you've gotten to this point and you've worked through some of your stuff, it's time for growth!

You are stronger now, more than you realize, and you are more equipped to handle the curveballs that life will throw your way—you have the ability to knock them out of the park and circle the bases too. It's time to reach higher heights!

Finding Your Mountain

Everyone has goals and dreams and things they want to achieve in life, and we climb many hurdles to get there—whether it's a dream job, promotion, new love, big house, or celebrity status. Whatever that is for you, we have to work, climb, jump over hurdles and through hoops to get there. It's a trek to say the least but a well-rewarded one. I like to visualize my trek as a mountain that I am climbing. Visualize it with me.

At the top of your mountain, you will find all of the goals and dreams that you've ever dreamt as you lay your head on your pillow at night. The path begins at the bottom of the mountain, and you have to climb to the top to get there. To accomplish these goals, the climb takes strength—physical and mental strength.

The mountain you are climbing to your goals—such as one might climb to reach a bachelor's, master's, doctorate degree, or successful business—is an opportunity to grow, create, and stretch yourself to new, exciting levels. But not everybody sees them that way because a mountain (a degree or business) can look intimidating, and it can feel overwhelming when you're standing on ground level looking up. That was the feeling I felt as I started my trek up a real mountain like Mount Whitney, the tallest mountain in the contiguous US (almost 15,000 feet). But I conquered it, one step at a time. So, I'm not just talking about climbing metaphorical mountains. When you build strength, you can climb real mountains too, or whatever you love to do.

That reminds me of the time when my three colleagues and I started the trek up Mount Whitney on a nice, sunny day. This was back when I was an accountant—I had discovered the power of working out, but I wasn't quite a fitness professional yet. Our plan wasn't to hike Mount Whitney all in one day; the first day, we only planned to reach about 4,000 to 7,000 feet in elevation. Before we even got there, a woman in our party started having headaches. It was because she was taking in less oxygen than normal. The air is thinner that high up, and she was dizzy. And dizzy is not a state you want to be in when you're carrying your tent, food, and a bunch of other stuff in your backpack. Did I mention I had never been camping before that trip?

There are serious risks with climbing that high. So, before we even set up camp for the night, this woman decided that she wasn't going to climb any higher. She knew that she wouldn't make it to the top. But when I walked out of my tent the next morning, I didn't feel like I had a choice. I hadn't come that far to quit. I was so close. This mountain wasn't just about climbing 15,000 feet. In my head, I knew I was pushing my limits, but I also knew I had to push my limits. How was I going to do that? You guessed it—one step at a time.

Whether you are climbing up the corporate ladder, building a new business, or trying to raise a family, there are steps you must take to reach these goals. Each step puts you higher on your personal mountain and closer to your goal at the top. To avoid being intimidated by the height of your plight (or your dream), celebrate yourself for completing each step, and your confidence will grow as you climb. We celebrated at certain points as we climbed higher up the mountain by doing a high five, eating trail mix or cheese and crackers, and drinking some H20.

Preparation is Key

Everybody starts their climb at ground zero, the bottom of the mountain. Your first step should be to *prepare* for the climb. It doesn't mean that you won't run into problems along the way, but it does mean you can handle them better, and it does mean that you will most likely be more successful at reaching the top.

Just like life itself, my climb up Mount Whitney was fun, but it was scary and dangerous too. It was tough, and there were a lot of twists and turns involved with climbing to the top. It was even life-threatening. You could fall off the cliff if you made one wrong move. I went the wrong way a few times and came to the edge of a cliff. The snow was an added danger. You could get attacked by a bear or hemorrhage from the brain because the air gets thinner the higher you go. You also run the risk of dehydrating. In fact, my girlfriend and I ran out of water and had also forgotten our water purifier.

I did some research, so I knew that headaches were a part of climbing mountains as high as Mount Whitney. I wanted to feel prepared. I needed to know the 4-1-1 on camping, climbing, and everything that comes with this type of trek. All of that information came in handy as I climbed higher and higher up the mountain.

When our colleague got a headache, I wasn't surprised. That is what altitude sickness will do to you. Altitude sickness was also hitting some guys along the trek that we saw puking their brains out near the last lake before the summit. Luckily, they gave us their water since they couldn't continue. I had read an entire book on altitude sickness before my trip—I knew what was coming. My research also told me how to protect myself when the symptoms started to hit me.

On my way up the mountain, my body started to feel out of control—it mimicked what they call a drunken stupor. It's due to thinning oxygen. And I knew if I pushed myself too hard without being safe, my brain would hemorrhage. I didn't want that. When my symptoms started to take hold, I went to a lower point in elevation to stabilize.

When I made decisions like this, I knew I had control. And that control came from confidence, and that confidence came from awareness, research, and good preparation. Making those decisions and having that confidence is so empowering. On the contrary, freaking out because you don't know how to deal with life's curveballs can cause issues. Who knows what would have happened if I hadn't read that book on climbing and altitude sickness?

I managed my symptoms appropriately all the way to the top of the mountain. The last 600 feet, in particular, were incredibly taxing; we had to pay extra attention to where we were hiking. Plus, it was getting dark by the time we reached the summit. So, we quickly took a few pictures, signed our names in the journal that was at the top of the mountain to document we were there and headed back.

The round trip took about ten hours. We were the last ones to make it! But I didn't care how fast I got there or how many people got there before me—I made it. I conquered it! The trek was brutal, and I knew that many people along the way didn't make it.

Now isn't that just the way life is? It has a lot of twist turns and dangers. Right? But let me tell you, the rewards are GREAT! It takes time, it takes nurturing, and it takes strategy, preparation, and focus. And when you take micro steps, it's manageable. So, keep that in mind when climbing for your real-life personal goals.

Climbing and Rerouting

People didn't believe I could climb Mount Whitney. People also didn't believe that I could climb many of the mountains in my life: changing jobs, finding love again, breaking world records. But I didn't listen to the naysayers. I didn't need them. I prepared by doing my research and relying on mentors along the way. With the right positive people in your life, you can climb any mountain and reach any goal you choose.

Where are you on your trek? Have you only taken one step up your personal mountain? Two steps? Three steps? Wherever you are is okay. As long as you are not standing still, you're on the right track. Take that climb one micro step at a time.

Here are a few rules that can help:

1. **Break it down**—The steps to your goal: What can you tackle this year? This month? Today? Right now? No mountain climber expects to run from base camp to the

peak in an hour. Break down what you can do today to take that first step up the mountain.

2. **Change your focus**—Avoid concentrating on the mountain top. When you focus on the furthest point or on the hardest part of your journey, you will feel defeated before you even start. Instead, break it down into daily tasks, and focus your energy on completing each micro step—one step at a time. For example: if you want to lose weight, your first micro step in your trek up your personal mountain would be to book an appointment with your doctor. The second step might be to get bloodwork done to check on the state of your general health. Next, in your third step up the mountain you might want to find out your deficiencies and follow the doctor's protocol to fix them. *(See the figure on page 202 to get a clear vision of how this mountain might look.)* Before you know it, you'll see that when you focus on the joy and satisfaction of completing each step, you'll be halfway up your mountain and closer to your goals. The same is true if you want to start a new business. The first step up your mountain might be to research the type of business you're interested in (like I did before climbing Mount Whitney). The second step may require going back to school or getting special training. Again, like magic, you'll reach summit before you know it.

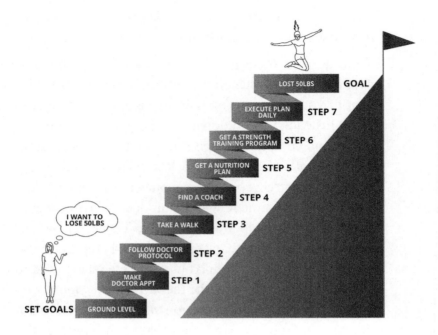

3. **Work at your own pace**—Our culture tries to hurry us along on their time schedule. All of our lifestyles are different. There is no one-size-fits-all. Figure out what works for your lifestyle and comfort level. Avoid comparing yourself to other people and social media expectations. Your progress is fine at the rate it happens. Avoid overnight success expectations generated by the media. It will eliminate false expectations and frustration.

4. **Reroute when necessary**—Is your climb going to be a straight path to the peak? Not always! You may have to adapt to new situations, and you may have unexpected detours.

   That's why I compare climbing an actual mountain to the real-life experiences of climbing to reach goals because I had a different view at every level while climbing Mount

Whitney and therefore made adjustments at every angle on the way to the top. Everyone on that mountain was doing the same thing. From the perspective of some, their decision was to retreat to rethink their next move.

The same is true while I was climbing to reach my personal life goals. There were times when I had to take steps back, reset my expectations, and fight the temptation to rush into my next moves. You will face this too. You just have to find a way to put one foot in front of the other. The more you do it and understand that we all falter, the farther you will go on your journey. That's what resilience is all about—pushing through slow and steady, never quitting.

If your intuition is telling you that you need to reroute, you're 100 percent correct. Don't doubt yourself or make excuses. Rerouting is a natural process. As you climb your personal mountain toward your life goals, you will view things differently at every level, so don't get married to one way of doing things. With each step, evaluate what you've done and adapt if you need to. Embrace the new perspective you gain as you climb up the mountain to your goal. It's essential to stay flexible and adapt when necessary to gain resilience.

When climbing your personal mountain, many long-lasting rewards will come with sowing and nurturing your own personal seeds at your own pace, versus watching someone else's pace. Trusting the daily process with a steady foot and consistent flow will help you develop the skills to adapt and change your perspective when necessary.

Reprogram your mind to think like a car navigation system. When you're driving and you make a wrong turn, your car will automatically recalculate and keep moving forward until it reaches its destination and so must you.

5. **Check in with yourself every day.** Ask, "Did I complete today's daily task?" If so, celebrate yourself with a pat on the back or something else that won't take away from your goal. Feel satisfied that you are on the right track and trust that you will arrive soon at the top of your personal mountain. To ensure accountability, have a coach or mentor help you keep track.

6. **Don't let your past failures turn you into a mushroom—** Just because you failed at something in the past doesn't mean you're a failure. Failure is a part of success. All winners have failed and made mistakes along the way. ALL! The most important thing to understand is that the only sure way to fail is to stop trying. Thomas Edison failed at doing 1,000 experiments until the 1,001 time he succeeded with the light bulb.

   See failure as a temporary setback. It can't hold you back from anything unless you let it. The *only* thing that can hold you back is what you tell yourself and what you believe. Daily affirmations will help you feed your mind positive data. Feeding yourself positive data daily creates resilience.

Keep Your Balance While Climbing: The Work-Life Challenge

Climbing your personal mountain is all about achieving life goals, but you have to show up as your best self to make that happen. And being your best self requires that you maintain a healthy work-life balance. Maintaining a healthy life balance is essential for happiness and well-being; it can also be a tremendous boost to all facets of your life, including productivity, career, business success, and relationships. A well-balanced person has a far greater ability to focus their attention and energy on attaining their goals, taking productive actions, and moving forward in a meaningful way.

To find that balance, it's important to first get clear on what better work-life balance means for you. Ask yourself—where am I off balance, and what are my priorities? Sit down and think about it.

- Are you pushing yourself harder at work versus not taking time for yourself to enjoy?
- Are you sedentary and eating extra goodies versus exercising, eating, and drinking healthy?
- Are you giving more love than receiving?
- Are you having too much fun while all else goes to hell?

If you are out of balance and one side of your life is more extreme than the other, work on fixing the imbalance.

After you've checked in with yourself, list your priorities, establish boundaries, set limits, and learn to say no to things that further push you away from your goals and out of balance with life. Also, set time limits on how much of your time you will give to others.

Let's face it. When you're trying to find balance in your life, things can get out of your control. You will have setbacks, there will be obstacles, you'll feel tired, lost and frustrated, and sometimes everything goes wrong all at once—everything! But don't throw in the towel. It's difficult when you are in the moment but with the things I've taught you so far, you can do it! See it as a test of strength! See it as a test of character! Know that it's only temporary, and you must fight through it. That is how I've survived so many storms. Just like you, I've had heartbreaks, job failures, and at times felt that I didn't measure up. I've made lots of mistakes climbing my personal mountains. There were times—many times—that I lost confidence and had accidents. I didn't even always make the right choices raising my kids. Encountering those setbacks sucked out my confidence, and it turned into a nasty cycle. People took advantage of me when they saw I was so low. That reminds me of the day I felt like my life literally went to hell in a handbasket.

I remember sitting at my desk at work trying to focus but having a hard time. The phone rings; I pick it up, it's the school . . . again! Apparently, my son is having temper tantrums, disrupting class, chewing gum, and talking back. The minute I get the call, I feel this anxiety go through my chest and into my throat, cramps grip my stomach, and chills run up my spine, because now I have to leave work and go take care of my child . . . AGAIN!

Oh, my goodness . . . how on earth am I going to keep a job with this continually going on? I care about my job, but I shouldn't even be caring or thinking about a job if my son is having problems at school. Surely, he is more important. I had to keep my job though, so we could eat and keep a roof over our head. But I'm not doing well at work either. I missed seventeen days already this month because of problems with my children, and now I've got to leave work again. If I were a good mother, that would be my priority, so I'm feeling guilty that I'm not making my kids my priority. I'm feeling guilty that I have to leave work too.

So, I finally pick up my son and learn he will have to be transferred out of that class. This is happening and then it's a fight at school. I'm concerned about how I would get there and how I will get back to work. I'm running low; do I have enough money to get gas and dinner too? From work to his school was thirty-five miles. By the time I get to bed at night, I'm an absolute mess. I'm exhausted, but I can't sleep. My sleep deprivation was often accelerated when my daughter was out late at night.

To add fuel to the fire, the next day, the emergency room called me. It was my daughter this time. She had been assaulted and was in bad shape. I had to leave work yet again. It was the worst possible time to leave work because it was month-end closing, but I had to go. I had been up all day and night in the emergency room. I had no sleep for twenty-four hours—but knew I needed to get back to work to try to save my job. Don't know how I got there. All I know is by 10:00 a.m., I was falling asleep with my eyes open. While I was in the middle of writing a report, I would just zone out. The pen made a line across the paper three times before I realized I couldn't think or function. It was horrible. I was falling out of my chair like I was drunk. I called for two family members to pick me up. Two because I could barely stand up so I certainly couldn't drive. The sad part is my boss believed none of it and wanted me to stay at work anyway. I was a wreck mentally, physically, and emotionally, and my life was out of balance.

But I'm here today because I pushed through every time. I broke that cycle of hopelessness and desperation, and I developed this attitude of gratitude. I'm not saying it was easy, but with repetition and time, I got stronger.

I also learned that even when things happen outside of your control, you still have control. You have control over how you respond to it, and you have control over the choices you make because of it.

Living out Loud

Pushing through the tough times is one thing. Meeting your goals is another. But it is even more exciting when you can exceed the limits and achieve your wildest dreams. Isn't that what living your best life is all about? It is for me, and if it is for you, it's time to practice the art of "Living out Loud." Living out loud means living your truth boldly and unapologetically. It means grabbing every opportunity that comes your way. It means saying YES even when fear stares you down and says you can't do it, but your intuition says YES YOU CAN!

If you want to live your truth, if you want to feel a joy that you can't explain, and if you want to empower yourself as you climb to the top of your personal mountain, you must first believe you can do it. You are far more capable than you think, and you can achieve everything you desire! The question is do you feel you deserve all you desire? Dig deep down into your soul and ask yourself whether you truly believe that you are worthy of having the things you desire in life. Do you believe you are worthy of that goal you set for yourself at the top of that mountain you are climbing? If your answer is no, beware as it could hinder your climb. But it's not too late. Now would be a good time to raise your "Deserve Level" to ensure a successful climb.

Raise Your Deserve Level

What is Deserve Level? Deserve level is the unseen force that shapes your life, for better or worse. What you truly feel and believe about yourself **determines what you will accomplish and have in every area of your life**.

Your whole life is run by what is stored in your unconscious mind. For example, if you say to yourself, "I'm a good person; I deserve to have a job that inspires me every day and pays me an incredible salary." Or maybe you think, "I'm a loving person; I deserve to have the relationship of my dreams." If you don't have them, it might be because you have a low Deserve Level in those areas. You will sabotage it all unconsciously. Your unconscious mind drives your conscious mind to action or inaction based on your deserve level.

Your value system was developed through a collection of life experiences—past and present—and those experiences get lodged in your unconscious. Your unconscious forms an opinion about yourself and your place in the world and gives you a rating of how deserving you are of whatever it is in life that you want. Like a computer, your unconscious self is programmed and running your life from behind the scenes with everything you think about yourself.

When we tell ourselves that we don't deserve the best, we accept less and less. We settle. We become content with mediocrity, routine, and complacency. We allow our self-esteem to take hit after hit, and it never really recovers. And your children and grandchildren take that same wand from living with you, and they too absorb that mentality.

So how do you raise your Deserve Level? You have to start by embracing you—every part of you! Believe that you are worthy because you are!

This Little Light of Mine

Living out loud is all about letting your light shine in your own unique way without shame or fear of judgment. Let it shine in a big way and stand loud and proud in your truth. Even when those around you are not shining brightly, never dim your light to help them shine. Never belittle yourself or cower down to make someone else feel good. Never make excuses or feel embarrassed about who you are. When you play yourself down, you can't live to your full potential or fulfill your ultimate purpose and you can't receive the joy you deserve.

Fill Your Cup and Pass It On

I believe we are here to make the world better and each one of us has a role in it. But it starts with each of us individually. That means you have to make yourself a priority. Take care of you first. Clean your house and put it in order before you can help or advise others. Fill your cup to the top by showering yourself with love, care, and things that spark joy for you; when your cup overflows, you'll naturally want to share it with others. It's the pond affect—a pebble thrown in the pond ripples out to the world.

Only after we are straight can we help the next person get straight and then they pass the baton to help the next. When that happens, they grow, you grow, and the world just gets better. I've been doing just that, and it's so rewarding. Let me tell you . . .

There was a woman named Sarah who desperately wanted to meet me and potentially work with me, but she wasn't sure how she could make it happen. She was plagued by family drama, medical issues, and working at a dead-end job she didn't like.

One day, she heard that I was coming into a town near her to speak at an event. She did everything possible to get a ticket to come and see me. She was willing to pay her dues and invest in herself.

As I was leaving at the end of the event, Sarah was also on her way out. We collided outside and before I got in the car, Sarah stopped me and said, "Look. I sold everything I had and took two weeks' pay just to get here because I wanted to see and hear from you in person." During my event, she had learned some lessons and told me exactly how she was going to apply them.

My response was, "Awesome! No one ever tells me that! They always say my events are great, but they don't tell me how they are going to apply what they learned. So, I said to Sarah, "I'll meet with you later today at 5:00 p.m., but I need you to do something crazy." She says, "What?" I said, "I'll meet with you, but I need you to wear a red hat." Crazy, right?

Sarah shows up at the right time and says, "Why do I have to wear this red hat?" I said, "Just because you took action, and you are willing to do something out of the ordinary, it shows me that you didn't show up (to meet my challenges) once, but you showed up twice. Now, I'm an open book. Tell me how I can help you?"

I decided to mentor Sarah. Over the years, I took her on a long journey of mentorship by coaching her, having her assist me at events, and introducing her to some of the people that influenced me. Sarah learned many of the same lessons, and now she's become very successful in her own right. She completely changed her life and her career and is very happy.

She's reported it all back to me. One of the last amazing things she communicated to me was this: She was away at an event and suddenly someone came up to her and asked, "How did you become so successful?" She said, "It's funny, and I'd love to tell you over lunch, but I need you to show up in a red hat."

Passing the baton is how the world turns. I just love it when that happens! When you are strong physically and mentally and you raise your deserve level, you can make a bigger impact on the world—one person at a time and one micro step at a time.

True Freedom

The next time you ask how I've achieved all that I have: "How did you climb to reach your goals, and how did you push through the hard times?" I'm going to hand you this book. I want you to understand the deeper meaning behind what it takes to get to where you want to go without quitting. And to know the whole truth. And the truth is, there was a time when I dimmed my light and ignored the gifts I had to share with the world. But after I found the courage to be me—game over! I never went back to that place again. Every day, I get up in the morning and live my truth. That's what I want for you. Now is the time to execute the gifts you were born with too.

"There is no passion to be found playing small—in settling for a life that is less than the one you are capable of living."
—Nelson Mandela

If you live in a cell of shame, secrecy, and fear, you can never be free. Risk stepping outside of your comfort zone, and you'll experience true freedom. Don't fall prey to doubts and insecurities by trying to clone others. You are the best *you* there could ever be. I had to tell myself the same thing when I think about some critical points in my life. I would say to myself, I've got to stop trying to fit the mold of everyone else—I'm Wendy Ida! And I'm the best Wendy Ida in the whole world. I'm enough because I am me. Repeat that phrase to yourself with your own name.

This realization set me free! It changed my life. I've never looked back. Your confidence and self-esteem rise, and you feel on top of the world. Suddenly, you have more energy to push for what you deserve. Every time I achieved a goal, I felt empowered to do more, risk more, and push my limits. Each time, I felt stronger, and not just physically. I felt stronger mentally and had more faith in myself despite the setbacks I had along the way. Each time I turned what I thought before was impossible to POSSIBLE! Life is a journey; each thing you do builds you up for the next thing to create and accomplish.

To this day, I continue to push my limits. I keep a childlike attitude; therefore, I think, feel, and have experienced that there aren't any limits. The sky is not even the limit. But that's the way you feel when you are diligent and consistent in climbing for your goals. It pays off! You get a sense of your personal power and know you deserve everything you get when you put in the work.

Everything I've talked about—from building resilience to moving through the Hallway to reclaiming your strength and opening your Safe Box—is meant to help you raise your deserve level and reach your true joy and purpose in life.

A Fighting Spirit

Through all of my experiences, I not only developed this attitude of gratitude, but I also developed this fighting spirit to help me push through fear or anytime things get tough. I use pain as motivation, fear as determination, and when someone says I can't do it, I gather my strength and push through to make my goal in spite of what they said. In my mind, "no" only means find another way to do it. The more I push through my obstacles the stronger I get, the more my faith is restored and the more I grow and learn and pass it on to others. YOU *have the same ability*!

Unleash your hidden warrior and use that fighting spirit to survive and thrive. You have the talent and you have a gift buried deep inside of you. You can soar among the stars and reach your highest potential and ultimate goals and dreams.

I challenge you to go out and *make a conscious shift* to push past your fears, live loud and proud, and do it unapologetically!

Micro Steps to Climbing Your Mountain

I made so many micro moves to climb to the top of Mount Whitney—the book I bought to prepare for the trip, the class I took, and every ounce of preparation contributed to my victory. I also made a lot of micro moves in my everyday life to ascend every other metaphorical mountain—like when I prepared for a bodybuilding competition, the Guinness World record, authoring other books such as, *Take Back Your Life, The Action Guide,* and *Habits of Success*, changing careers and opening my own coaching and training business, and even pushing through my fears in the Hallways of my life. Now, it's time for you. Take the bull by the horns and go for it!

Just like if you're going to climb a real mountain like Mount Whitney, you will need to train. You don't just say, "I'm going to Everest today. See you tomorrow!" The same idea applies to all of your other life goals, whether it's body goals, losing weight, a big bank account, a loving relationship, flourishing career, a big house, a nice car, nice clothes—part of preparing is understanding that some parts of your climb will be steeper than others. Sometimes, the footing is treacherous; sometimes, you may be worried about falling back. Those times are worth the extra effort when you hit a more level stretch where you can enjoy the scenery—like taking a breath and being proud of how far you've come. And the way that you will get there is by never giving up.

When you complete these micro moves and build strength little by little, you won't want to give up. Stay focused, stay healthy, put one foot in front of the other, and have some fun along the way to the mountain top.

Envision Your Mountain

What does your personal mountain look like? Describe it. Describe how you will feel at the top and the achievements that will get you there. This is all a part of the preparation you need to move upward. With your mountain in mind, write down how you will get there. Spend some time every day planning your micro moves:

- List your goals and priorities.

- Break down in detail what you need to do each day to climb your mountain.

- Create a graphic vision board of a mountain with your goal star at the top.

- Label the steps up the mountain (daily and weekly things to do).

- Reward yourself.

- Write down how you will take your first step upward today.

- Write down how you will show up and show out for yourself.

- Write down three to five other things that will happen, whether they will directly help you up your mountain or help you build strength and resilience for your journey ahead.

- Once you write these tasks down, activate them. Repeat and review daily.

Strengthen Your Spirit with Me Time

When planning your day and your trek up your personal mountain to reach your goals, consider where and when you are going to have "me time." Take just five minutes each day for "me time." Use this structure to do things that strengthen your spirit and take care of yourself:

- Breath work

- Self-Reflection

- A workout

- Eating a nutritious meal

◆ Repeating kind and powerful phrases to yourself in the mirror

Challenge yourself to take this "me time" every day. I know it doesn't seem like much—but that's what micro moves are all about. Every minute you spend nourishing yourself will get embedded into your soul. It will affect the way you work, sleep, and play. Climbing toward your goals will be much easier when you feel great, sleep well, and have the strength to push forward.

Practice That Gratitude

"Me time" can also be five minutes of daily gratitude. If you woke up today, don't wake up angry. Waking up is already one thing to be grateful for. It's a good day to continue the climb toward your goals. If you woke up today, it's a good day to keep moving forward on this journey called life. What else can you think of as you go about your day?

No matter where you are in your climb toward your goals, you can highlight the positives. Before going to bed, list five to ten positive things that happened throughout the day. Did you accomplish the five micro moves you set out to do that day? Be grateful. Staying positive and upbeat leaves you open to new ideas, opportunities, and learning experiences. Being negative forces you to stew in your own bitter juices and ruins your health, like a slow death. Take some action every day to make your day a little brighter.

Remember, the goal of these micro moves is to help you understand that the climb to your goals is not a big scary animal waiting to devour you at the top. Everything you desire when taken in bite-size pieces can be a rewarding trip filled with the love, care, and respect you deserve.

Believe that you are worthy of royalty! Believe that you are worthy of seeing the world at your feet! Believe that you deserve all you desire! It is your birthright! Understand, however, that you've got to work for it, and it *will* get uncomfortable. Use the skills you were born with and what you've learned along the way. Then SMILE, and it will be all good!

Next Steps

"Let your dreams be bigger than your fears, your actions louder than your words, and your faith stronger than your feelings."
—Nicky Gumbel

Life on the Other Side

Just like I passed the baton to Sarah, JJ, Vincent, Carol, Bonnie, and all of my clients, I now want to pass the baton to you. Take it and run! Be all you were born to be and all you are capable of. Life is too short to do anything else. I've shared tools, moves, and encouragement to help you go forward, be yourself, and work your magic. I'm confident that you now have the skills to move through any Hallway, climb any mountain, and get back up again and again anytime you fall, even when life has humbled you to your knees. You *will be* tested—that you can count on—and when you are tested, proudly use the skills you've developed here.

The Good Stuff Takes Time

I didn't escape an abusive situation on my first try. I didn't lose eighty pounds overnight. When I climbed Mount Whitney, I was the last person to make it to the top and the last person to crawl into my tent that night. I made strides and achieved what I wanted amid the distractions and despite the obstacles and negative chatter along the way. Our culture reinforces impatience. They spread false ideas of overnight success and tell us that people became successful without showing us the work that went into that success. It's essential that you unhook your expectations from the false narratives and clickbait headlines that hurry you along and tell you that you're not moving fast enough. You are going at exactly the rate you should be going. If you read one chapter today, celebrate! If you took one walk around the block today, celebrate! Every micro move I shared in this book is bringing you closer to the person you have always wanted to be. Trust yourself. Stick to your guns. Go at your own pace and keep putting one foot in front of the other.

Don't Judge Yourself

Avoid comparing yourself to other people along the way. Everyone starts at a different point. Regardless of your age or what point you are starting from, it's okay to find joy in the process and be proud of yourself for everything that you are doing to improve your life. Don't let anyone shame you into thinking you are boasting or, on the contrary, you should measure up to their standards. Also, skip past the social media posts that entice you to compare yourself with them. Just do what you have to do to avoid looking at where everyone else is on their journey.

Even now, I have moments where I'm not as far along as the people next to me or I fall short and that's okay. I'm still me, and I'm still moving forward, having fun and loving myself every step of the way!

Never Give Up!

They say when it rains, it pours—true! My client repeated that to me the other day when she explained why she had to cancel some sessions and take a couple weeks off. Her cat died, then she cracked her tooth followed by surgery. The pandemic years, combined with other stressful family and personal issues, have put all of my fighting skills to the test. I'm sure they have put you to the test as well. As I've said before, Hallways will continue. In fact, I had finalized my thoughts in this chapter and was ready to print, until I received an email from my wonderful editor, Wendy Hall, that said, "My dear Wendy, I enjoyed working with you so much. My husband was tragically killed in an explosion two days ago. I have no idea how I will cope or handle this, but I am taking time off from work. I hope your book turns out perfect!!!" *What?* I couldn't comprehend or digest that. Shock and crying like a baby are all I remember. While I'm honored that she took time to write me and wish me well at this time in her life, it speaks volumes of her character and I know she will go on to live a great life.

Every one of us has a story and we must continue to fight through it. We have needed more emotional and mental support than ever! How I have gotten through this time, for both myself and my clients, is having a fighter mentality. I fight for myself, I fight for my family, and I fight for my clients—it's a calling. It's why I get up in the morning, it's why I climbed the personal mountains in my life to achieve the goals and dreams that make me happy, and it's why I wrote this book. I'm fighting for you. You must fight for yourself too!

When you feel like giving up, remind yourself of why you started in the first place, and it will motivate you to keep going. Why did you take this journey? Who is it for? What gets you out of bed in the morning? Make sure the reason you started this journey is a strong one so you can use it as fuel to continue to fight and rise above when life knocks you down.

It reminds me of what I always hear Kendall Toole, a Peloton instructor, say, "You can knock me down, but you can't knock me out!" I live by that motto because I know after the dust settles, I will rise back up and recreate myself. In my favorite poem by Maya Angelou called, *Still I Rise*. She says, *"You may write me down in history / with your bitter, twisted lies, / You may trod me in the very dirt / but still, like dust, I'll rise."* Her words give me power, and they reinforce my Wendy Warrior fighting spirit!

Find or create a mantra or personal slogan you can say aloud for that extra pick-me-up to help you gain that fighting spirit to push through whatever you're going through.

Resilience is all about rising every time you fall. Make a promise to yourself. Challenge yourself! Look fear in the eyes—Face Everything And RISE! Don't stop until you reach the top!

As you develop into a resilient being, you gain positive traits like emotional well-being, inner drive, future focus, and physical health. With each positive step you take toward becoming more resilient, your confidence grows and therefore, you take more risks. Your energy increases and you want to do more, be more, and take care of yourself better. This keeps you motivated, hopeful, and excited for your future.

I vow every time to rise. I vow every time to fight! I vow every time to *never give up*! I extend my hand to you so you can do the same.

Now you know what to do. Go do it!

7 TIPS TO LOOKING FIT FIERCE, AND FABULOUS

Includes: 7 Minute Circuit Workout

GIVE ME 20 MINUTES
AND I'LL GIVE YOU THE TOOLS NEEDED TO TAKE YOUR BODY AND LIFE TO THE NEXT LEVEL.

I created this e-book and video because I want to help others improve their lives, live their dreams and serve the world through their passion. To make the kind of impact I'm talking about and to serve a greater good, it's important that you be **FIT, FIERCE, AND FABULOUS!**

This FREE e-book and video could be a blessing in disguise! You can't afford not to know this. You have to take action to make things happen!

https://bit.ly/FitFierceFabulous

About the Author

Wendy Ida *(ee'da)*, also known as "America's #1 Expert on Living Fit, Fierce & Fabulous after 40," is an internationally recognized best-selling author, speaker, TV host, lifestyle coach, and fitness expert. She is also a two-time Guinness World Record holder, eight-time award-winning National Fitness Champion, and former Assistant Strength and Conditioning Coach for the LA Avengers football team.

Wendy won the Indie literary award for her book, *Take Back Your Life: My No Nonsense Approach to Health, Fitness and Looking Good Naked*—foreword by Les Brown, motivational speaker, and her book *Habits of Success* is a *USA Today* and *Wall Street Journal* best seller. Wendy has made dozens of appearances on TV, talk radio, and other media such as *Essence Magazine, The Dr. Oz Show, Inside Edition, CNN, Fox Sports Network, NBC, ABC, BET*, commercials, exercise videos, and more.

She has toured with actors and producers Boris Kodjoe and Nicole Ari Parker as their "Strive to Thrive" fitness expert and was also Director of the Obesity Prevention Initiative Program in association with USC Norris Comprehensive Cancer Center, Kaiser Permanente, American Bio-Clinical Laboratories, and the RMCF.

Twice nominated for Who's Who among Women in Business, Wendy Ida also received the Award of Recognition for Outstanding

Educational Community Service from Dr. Charles Adams, founder and president of the Educational Outreach Community Program.

New Jersey-born Wendy Ida says she didn't start working out until age forty-three but managed to improve her health, lose eighty pounds, dwindle down to a rock-solid size four, and hold on to it as a grandmother!

Wendy teaches, preaches, and inspires others to reinvent their lives and live their potential through mental readiness, self-worth, and physical challenges. Wendy says, "My mission to change lives around the world is what gets me out of bed in the morning."

Contact her at https://linktr.ee/WendyIda.

Printed in Great Britain
by Amazon

19472029R00140